S9

1st ed

1477

8 00

YOUR NIGHT
TO MAKE DINNER

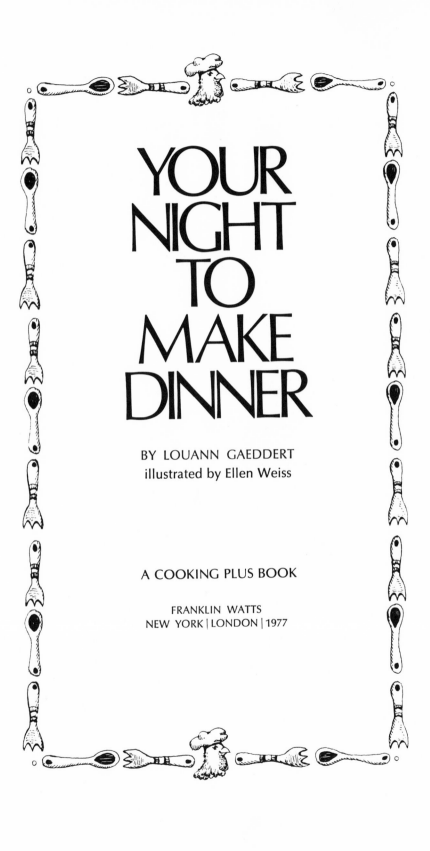

YOUR NIGHT TO MAKE DINNER

BY LOUANN GAEDDERT
illustrated by Ellen Weiss

A COOKING PLUS BOOK

FRANKLIN WATTS
NEW YORK | LONDON | 1977

Library of Congress Cataloging in Publication Data

Gaeddert, LouAnn Bigge.
    Your night to make dinner.

        (A Cooking plus book)
        Includes index.
        SUMMARY: Includes time saving and budget
recipes for a variety of dishes and tips on meal
planning, shopping, cooking safety, and nutrition.
        1.   Cookery—Juvenile literature.   [1.   Cook-
ery]   I.   Weiss, Ellen.   II.   Title.
TX652.5.G33   641.5   77–5116
ISBN 0–531–01297–2

CONTENTS

TO MY DAUGHTER MARTHA,
AN EXCELLENT TEEN-AGE COOK,
WITH THANKS FOR HER HELP
IN PREPARING THIS BOOK

YOUR NIGHT
TO MAKE DINNER

KITCHEN CHANGES AND CHALLENGES

Because family life is changing, more and more teen-agers are cooking. Not just the occasional batch of fudge, but complete meals. If both of your parents hold full-time jobs, you may be totally responsible for your own breakfasts and lunches. This book contains two short chapters devoted to these meals with the emphasis on speed and nutrition. You may also be responsible for some or many family dinners. The main focus of this book is on the evening meal. The busier the family members, the more important the dinner hour—not only as a time for sharing wholesome food, but also as a time for sharing experiences and keeping in touch.

Fortunately, it's easy to learn to cook. The beginning violinist produces nothing but squeaks, the beginning typist produces lines of meaningless letters, but the beginning cook can produce a tasty meal on the first try. The super-simple main dish recipes in this book are marked **O**. If you have never cooked before, start with these. Budget recipes are marked **$**.

As with most skills, pleasure increases with ability. Once you have mastered basic cooking techniques, you can go on to more complicated recipes. You will eventually want to create your own dishes. Cooking, therefore, need never be boring or repetitious.

Finally, cooking is appreciated. Everyone enjoys a good meal, including you.

No matter how much you enjoy cooking, time will frequently be at a premium. The recipes in this book are arranged according to the time they take to prepare. All of the main dishes in chapter 1 can be prepared in 30 minutes. Other chapters are devoted to main dishes that can be prepared for the oven and ignored and more complicated dishes that can be prepared in advance for several meals. Each main-dish recipe is followed by a suggested menu. The book also contains chapters of suggestions for side dishes—vegetables, salads, starches, and desserts.

If the kitchen is like a foreign country to you, begin with a conducted tour. Find out where utensils are stored. Learn to operate your appliances safely.

Before you begin to prepare a recipe, read it all of the way through and assemble all of the ingredients. If the oven is to be preheated, turn it on about 15 minutes before you wish to use it. Follow the recipe carefully the first time. Remember that ovens vary so that the baking time may be either shorter or longer than indicated in the recipe. Tastes and appetites vary, too. Use file cards to copy the recipes you want to repeat. Jot down any adjustments you think are needed. If you think it needs more salt, say so. If you have leftovers, make a note to decrease the recipe.

Unless otherwise noted, all of the dinner recipes are designed to serve four hungry people. If you have a smaller or larger family, make appropriate adjustments. Most breakfast and lunch recipes are for single servings.

You will notice that metric measures are given in parentheses in every recipe. There is some confusion about how American cooks will use the metric system when it becomes commonplace. Will we, for example, translate 1 cup to 240 milliliters or to .24 liters? Or will we round it out to ¼ liter? Will we measure flour by weight as the Europeans do, or will we continue to measure flour in a cup? I have used milliliters instead of fractions of liters and I have assumed that Americans will continue to measure dry ingredients in a cup.

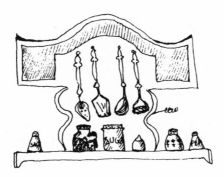

SAFETY TIPS

1.   To avoid burning your hands, use potholders. Drain foods cooked in boiling water into a colander or large sieve.

2.   Pare vegetables away from you. Slice or chop vegetables on a board.

3.   Turn handles of cooking utensils toward the back of the stove, not into the room where someone might bump into them.

4.   If grease should catch fire on your stove, *do not pour water on the flame.* Put it out with a CO_2 or dry chemical extinguisher. Use the extinguisher carefully so as not to spread the flames. If the fire is in a pan, put a heavy lid on it to smother the flames. Or pour baking soda over the flames. If the fire should spread beyond the pan, leave the house and call the fire department.

BEGIN WITH A PLAN

Happy dinner hours don't just happen. They require a plan. Begin with a family conference to decide who will do what when. Will the cooking be divided on a weekly basis? A daily basis? Will the person who gets home first start the dinner to be relieved by another member of the family? Who will set the table? Who will wash the dishes? Who will do the shopping?

Also discuss family finances. What you choose to cook must relate to the amount of money there is to spend. Perhaps your family has no money problems. In that unlikely event, you will probably rely on quickly prepared but expensive meats, and packaged and frozen delicacies. More probably, it will be necessary for you to strike some kind of a balance between luxury and economy meals. If you serve roast beef on Tuesday, you will serve tuna on Wednesday. Or you may be one of the millions who find it necessary to budget carefully at all times, either to make ends meet or to save money for a special project. Budget main dishes—generally speaking those that cost less than 40 cents a serving at today's prices in the Northeast—are identified to make them easy to spot. Remember that eating economically does not mean eating poorly—you just need to plan a little harder to eat well.

[4]

Variety is the key to interesting meals. Discuss what you are going to eat during the following week or two. Imagine the boredom if you, your brother, and your father all decide to cook hamburgers on consecutive nights! Beef is the all-American meat but try not to serve it two nights running. Plan instead to serve beef twice during the week. Serve chicken, fish, a meatless dish, pork, lamb, or veal on the other nights.

Consider variety, too, when planning individual menus. Variety of color, texture, and flavors. Consider this menu: veal stew, buttered noodles, creamed cauliflower, banana and cottage cheese salad, and custard. White and mushy! Now consider this: veal stew, buttered noodles, green beans, raw carrots and celery, and raspberry sherbet. The second menu is actually easier to prepare and less expensive than the first—and so much more appetizing.

Following are some meal planning dos and don'ts:

DO serve meat or another protein-rich dish and two or more vegetables at every dinner. Also serve a starch—potato, rice, pasta, or bread—to all but strict dieters. Unless you regularly eat fruit for breakfast, lunch, and snacks, serve it for dinner often.

DO try to include something green and something yellow, red, or orange with every main course. Not only will this assure an attractive plate, but it will also assure a nutritionally balanced meal.

DO strive for contrast. If one dish is bland, another should be tart; if one is creamy, another should be crunchy.

DON'T repeat flavors. If you are serving a vegetable in a cheese sauce, don't put blue cheese in the salad dressing.

DO serve only one gravy or sauce at a meal. Two sauces make for sloppy plates.

DO keep a supply of pickles and/or spiced fruit in the refrigerator to add sparkle to an otherwise drab plate. Warmed-over tuna looks festive if accompanied by a spiced apple ring. Carrots and radishes are also good "sparklers" as are sprinklings of parsley and paprika. Attractive food tastes better.

DO try to expand your tastes. Try new foods, new combinations. Be daring.

SHOPPING SENSE

Who will shop and how often depends on how well you plan, how busy you are, the distance to the grocery store, and how much storage and freezer space is available in your home.

When several people are sharing the cooking, a list becomes one of the most important items in the kitchen. Keep pencil and paper handy so that the person who uses the last pinch of oregano can write oregano on the list.

Consult newspaper ads for weekly specials. Time was when thrifty mothers spent hours driving from one store to another looking for the best prices. Few people today have the time for that. On any given shopping day, go to the supermarket that you like best or to the one that offers the greatest number of specials of interest to you.

Adjust your menu plans to fit the specials. Suppose you are planning to prepare roast pork and cauliflower but find that roast veal and broccoli are on sale. Change the menu.

If you have plenty of storage space, buy staple items—flour, sugar, coffee, rice, and so forth—when they are on special. Also stock up on specials from the freezer and the canned food shelves.

Generally speaking, big is better, but not always. Read the

unit pricing labels to be sure that you are really saving money when you buy the "giant economy size" of anything. Two smaller packages of an item on sale may be cheaper than one larger package of an item at the regular price. Buy new products, seldom-used items, and unfamiliar brands in small quantities. The greatest waste of all is to buy items and then not use them.

The vegetable chapter that begins on page 58 gives tips for buying fresh vegetables and tells when to buy frozen or canned rather than fresh. In-season fruit is always tastier and less expensive than out-of-season fruit, so when a fruit is in season buy as much of it as your family will eat. At other times, rely on canned fruit. Fruit varies greatly from brand to brand so shop carefully.

You may need to make extra trips to the store to buy milk. These trips can be avoided if your family will drink milk made from the dried product. Here again brands vary so buy small packages of "instant" milk until you find a product that pleases you. And serve it very cold. Fresh milk, eggs, and other dairy products are dated in many parts of the country. Check the dates carefully and buy the freshest product available, fre-

quently to be found at the back of the dairy case. Never buy a product after the expiration date.

Meat, poultry, and fish are the most difficult foods to buy and represent the largest percentage of the food dollar. It is disappointing to buy a steak that looks terrific in the package but is mostly bone on the underside. The only protection against this disappointment is to shop where you have been pleased with the meat in the past. If you need help, don't be afraid to ask the advice of the butcher. Following are a few general guides to different kinds of meat.

BEEF should be red or purple with white—not yellow—fat.

HAMBURGER or chopped beef contains more fat than chopped chuck, sirloin, or round and will shrink when broiled or fried. It is perfectly acceptable for spaghetti sauce or casseroles but you may not find it satisfactory for hamburgers.

VEAL should be delicate tan, not bright pink.

LAMB is being imported from New Zealand and Australia these days. I find imported lamb to be of a stronger, less pleasing flavor than domestic lamb, which is usually more expensive.

CHICKENS weighing 3 lbs. are a much better buy than bony little 2-lb. birds.

Once you've completed your shopping, head for home. Do not stop to chat with a friend or to buy a sweater. Do that on your way *to* the store. Proper storage is just as important as careful shopping. Refrigerate dairy products and fresh produce as quickly as possible. Get frozen foods back in the freezer before they thaw. Open plastic bags of potatoes and onions and store in a cool, dry place. Take meat that is to be used within a day or two out of the plastic wrap and rewrap it loosely in waxed paper so that air can circulate around it. Put it in the coldest part of your refrigerator. All other meats should be given a second airtight wrapping. Just place the plastic-wrapped meat into a plastic storage bag and close it tightly. Mark it so that you can see what it is, and write the date on it. Place in the freezer to be used within a month or so.

SPEEDY SPECIALS

You have track practice or guitar lessons on your day to prepare dinner? Help is here. All of the main dishes and menus in this chapter can be prepared in half an hour or less. Most are very easy. Although steak and veal cutlets are expensive, many of these recipes are also easy on the budget.

o   BROILED STEAK

The most difficult part of a steak dinner is shopping for the steak. There are so many kinds from which to choose. Select chuck, sirloin, strip, fillet, porterhouse, or T-bone. Do not select anything marked pepper steak or Swiss steak. If in doubt, ask the butcher. Buy 1½ to 2 lbs. (.7 to .9 kg) boneless steak or 3 to 4 lbs. (1.3 to 1.8 kg) steak with bone.

1.   First turn on the broiler. Then place the steak on a greased rack in a shallow pan.
2.   Figure out how long you think it is going to take to cook the steak. Most steak will require about 5 minutes on each side to reach the rare stage. A very thin steak will take about 4 minutes

on each side. A thicker steak will take longer and, of course, any steak will take longer if you wish it to be well-done, up to 10 minutes on each side.

3.   Count back from the dinner hour and, at the appropriate time, place the steak 3 inches (75 mm) from the flame or heating unit. Broil 5 minutes more or less; turn over and broil another few minutes. Remove from the oven and stick the point of a sharp knife into the center of the steak to see if it has reached the doneness you like. If not, return it to the broiler. If it is brown on the outside, but not done on the inside, lower the broiling pan and continue to cook.

4.   Season with salt and pepper after the broiling is complete.

London Broil is a very thick steak, about 2 inches (50 mm), which will take up to 25 minutes to reach medium-rare. When it reaches the degree of doneness you like, remove it from the oven and slice it thinly across the grain. (See illustration.)

Minute Steaks are put through a machine to make them tender. Pan-broil in salt as for hamburgers.

Serve steak with french fried or mashed potatoes, broiled tomatoes, a green salad, and cookies.

Hamburgers, by any other name, are still the staple American meat. A "giant quarter-pound burger" is mighty small, so allow ⅓ lb. (.15 kg) of ground beef—chuck is a good choice—for each person. Shape into patties about ½-inch thick (12 mm). *Handle lightly* and as little as possible. Do *not* squeeze and mash the meat into solid lumps.

To broil place on a greased rack, 3 inches (75 mm) below the heat. Broil for 5 minutes, turn the patties, and broil another 5 minutes. (If you like very rare meat, cook less time; if very well-done meat, cook longer.) When done, sprinkle with salt and pepper and serve.

To pan-broil, sprinkle salt in a skillet big enough to hold the number of patties you are cooking. Use about ¼ tsp (1 ml) salt per patty. Heat the skillet and add the patties. Cook over moderately high heat for about 5 minutes on each side.

Serve hamburgers with toasted English muffins, greens with assorted cold vegetables, potato sticks, and pears with ice cream and butterscotch sauce.

or

Serve Salisbury steak with sautéed mushrooms and onions, green beans with almonds, hard rolls, and a fruit cup.

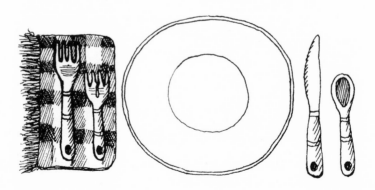

O   LAMB PATTIES AND PEACHES

> 1 to 1½ lbs. (.45 to .65 kg) ground lamb shaped into 4 patties
> 4 canned peach halves
> Salt
> Pepper
> Mint jelly

1.   Broil patties for a total of 10 minutes in a preheated broiler, or pan-broil in a heavy skillet or an electric skillet. (See Hamburgers.)
2.   Add peach halves (hollow side up) during the last 2 minutes, just to heat through.
3.   Sprinkle the patties with salt and pepper. Just before serving, spoon mint jelly into the peach halves.

Serve with creamed potatoes and peas, raw celery sticks, and chocolate cake.

O   VEAL SCALLOPS

> 4 veal scallops (thinly sliced cutlets), about 1 lb. (.45 kg)
> 2 tbsp (30 ml) margarine or oil
> Salt and pepper
> Juice of ½ lemon (optional)

1.   Wipe the scallops with a paper towel so they will brown well.
2.   Heat the margarine in a large skillet and add the scallops. Keep the fat hot but not burning. Sauté the scallops 3 to 4 minutes on one side and turn and brown another 3 to 4 minutes until tender on the other side. Add more fat if necessary. Sprinkle with salt and pepper.

3.   If you choose to use the lemon, put the scallops on a plate and pour any fat out of the skillet. Add the juice to the skillet and stir up any brown particles. Bring the juice just to the boil. Pour over the scallops.

Serve with rice, beets, green salad, and strawberry ice cream.

---

o   **INSTANT ELEGANCE**

Veal scallops prepared according to recipe above without the lemon juice.
1 5-oz. (140 g) can mushroom slices, drained
½ cup (120 ml) heavy cream or commercial sour cream

1.   Leave the finished scallops in the skillet to sprinkle with salt and pepper. Add mushrooms and cream. Heat but *do not boil.*

Serve with buttered noodles, asparagus, sliced tomatoes and cucumbers on greens, and raspberry sherbet with fresh or frozen raspberries. This is a menu worthy of your wealthy aunt and can be prepared in twenty minutes.

---

o   **FISH AND CHEESE BAKE**

---

4 serving-size pieces of fish—fillet of sole or flounder, hali-but, scrod, or other boneless, white fish
1 10½ oz. (297 g) can condensed cream of cheese soup
¼ cup (60 ml) bread crumbs, cracker crumbs, or corn flake crumbs

1.   Grease a flat casserole or 8-inch (20.3 cm) square baking dish generously.
2.   If your fish comes in fairly thick pieces, put them directly

into the casserole. If you have very thin fillets, fold them skin side in, to make neat packages. Try not to overlap the fish pieces.

3. Spoon the cheese soup over the fish. Sprinkle with crumbs.
4. Bake in a 350°F (175°C) oven about 20 minutes. Fish cooks very quickly. To test for doneness, push a few of the crumbs aside and put a fork down into a thick portion of the fish. The fish should come apart in flakes as you move the tines of the fork.

Serve with boiled whole potatoes with parsley, corn, cabbage slaw with apples, raisins and pineapple, and cake with mint topping.

Note: In this and other recipes calling for canned soup, use the standard 10½ oz. (297 g) size.

O $ **STUFFED FRANKFURTERS**

Frankfurters
American cheese
Sweet pickles
Bacon

1.   Split the frankfurters lengthwise almost in half. Cut the cheese and pickles into thin slices that will fit in the frankfurters. Wrap each in ½ slice bacon, securing the bacon with toothpicks.
2.   Place the frankfurter, cut side up, on a rack (you may use your broiling pan) in a pan. Bake in a 425°F (220°C) oven until bacon is crisp, about 10 minutes.

Serve with baked beans, cabbage slaw, and fruit cobbler.

O $ **HOT DOG TOWERS AND PEACHES**

8 frankfurters
1-lb. (.45 kg) can sauerkraut
6 servings instant mashed potatoes
¼ cup (60 ml) butter or margarine, melted
4 peach halves, well drained

1.   Split the frankfurters lengthwise almost in half so they will lie flat and place in a baking pan.
2.   Drain the sauerkraut well and spoon some on top of each frankfurter. Top with mashed potatoes and dribble butter over the top.
3.   Place peaches around the "towers" and bake in a 400°F (200°C) oven for 10 minutes, until the potatoes are lightly browned.

Serve with zucchini, hard rolls, and chocolate pudding.

[16]

$ **BACONY CHICKEN LIVERS**

2 slices bacon, cut in squares
1 lb. (.45 kg) chicken livers
Flour
Margarine
¼ cup (60 ml) chopped onion
1 cup (240 ml) water
1 chicken bouillon cube or 1 envelope instant chicken broth
Salt
Pepper

1. Fry the bacon and remove with a slotted spoon to a piece of paper towel.
2. Dip the livers in flour and fry quickly in the bacon fat. If necessary, add margarine. When the livers are brown and crispy, remove.
3. Add the onion and sauté briefly. Add more margarine so that there will be 1 tbsp (15 ml) in the skillet. Stir in 1 tbsp (15 ml) flour and allow to bubble briefly. Add the water, mixed with the bouillon cube, and stir until thickened.
4. Add the livers and cook in the sauce until hot and tender. This will take only a few minutes. Taste for seasoning. Top with bacon.

Serve with rice, carrots, bean salad, and lemon pudding.

$ **BACON AND EGG SPAGHETTI**

I first ate this dish at a tiny restaurant in Rome. On the same night, I saw the ruins of Rome by moonlight. That is one reason that this is my all-time-favorite recipe. Another reason is that it is the perfect "emergency" dinner—fast, economical, and delicious. It is also easy to multiply or divide to serve any number of people.

8 oz. (224 g) spaghetti, uncooked
8 slices bacon, each cut into four pieces
4 eggs
4 tsp (20 ml) milk
½ tsp (2.5 ml) salt
Few grinds pepper
Grated Parmesan cheese

1.   Cook the spaghetti according to the package directions, and fry the bacon. When the bacon is crisp, leave it in the skillet with the bacon grease.
2.   In the meantime, beat the eggs with the milk, salt, and pepper.
3.   When the spaghetti is tender, drain it quickly and return it to the pot in which it was cooked. Quickly pour the bacon and bacon fat and the egg mixture over the hot spaghetti and toss with a fork. If the spaghetti is hot enough, it will cook the eggs. If not, turn the heat on low and toss the spaghetti until the eggs are just barely creamy. Spoon ¼ cup (60 ml) cheese into the spaghetti. Pass the cheese at the table so that each person may add more.

Serve with a tossed vegetable salad, toast or French bread, and fresh fruit and cookies.

You rush home from a late play practice, throw your books wherever you usually throw them, rush to the kitchen, and then realize that you forgot to pick up the key ingredient for the dinner you were planning. Panic? Not if you have stocked up for just such an emergency. The following four recipes are all made from ingredients that can sit around waiting to rescue you. They are also super-fast and super-simple.

---

o   ## SALMON OR TUNA WEDGES

---

2 eggs

1-lb. (.45 kg) can salmon or 2 7-oz. (about .40 kg total) cans tuna

1 cup (240 ml) cracker crumbs

1 can condensed vegetarian vegetable soup

1.   Beat the eggs in a mixing bowl and add all of the other ingredients. (Crumb the crackers in the blender or put them in a plastic bag and roll them with a rolling pin.)

2.   Pour the mixture into a well-greased 8-inch (20 cm) pie plate. Bake 25 minutes in a 350°F (175°C) oven until the loaves are lightly browned and firm.

Serve with creamed potatoes, celery strips, and lemon pie.

---

o   ## HAM OR LUNCHEON MEAT WITH
SWEET POTATOES AND PINEAPPLE

Canned ham or luncheon meat (or leftover ham)

Canned sweet potatoes

Pineapple rings

About ½ cup (120 ml) brown sugar

About ¼ cup (60 ml) butter

1.   Cut ham or luncheon meat in serving-size pieces. Place in a lightly buttered shallow baking dish.
2.   Surround with canned sweet potatoes and pineapple rings. Sprinkle brown sugar on top and dot with butter.
3.   Bake 20 minutes in a 350°F (175°C) oven.

Serve with cabbage in cheese sauce, and brownies.

O   **HURRY-UP ONE-POT CHICKEN DINNER**

---

1 can condensed chicken-rice soup
1 can condensed cream of celery or cream of chicken soup
1 16-oz. (.45 kg) can of chow mein vegetables
1 7-oz. (.20 kg) can chicken or 1 cup (240 ml) cooked chicken
2 tbsp (30 ml) soy sauce
1 small box or can of chow mein noodles, about 2½ oz. (70 g)

1.   In a well-buttered casserole, mix together all of the ingredients except the noodles. Sprinkle the noodles on top.
2.   Bake in 350°F (175°C) oven until bubbly, about 25 minutes.

Serve tomato juice as a first course and fruit and cheese for dessert.

O $ **EMERGENCY FILLER-UPPER**

This recipe serves two, but it can easily be doubled or tripled. Great for crowds.

1 15- to 16-oz. (about .45 kg) can chili with beans
4 slices American cheese
4 toaster corn muffins or slices of white or whole wheat bread

1. Empty the chili into a saucepan and heat, stirring often.

2. Lay the cheese slices over the chili and cover. Simmer a few more minutes until the cheese begins to melt.

3. While the chili is simmering, toast the muffins or bread. Spoon the chili over the muffins, lifting the cheese carefully so that most of it lands on the top.

Serve with green salad, pickles, and fruit and cookies.

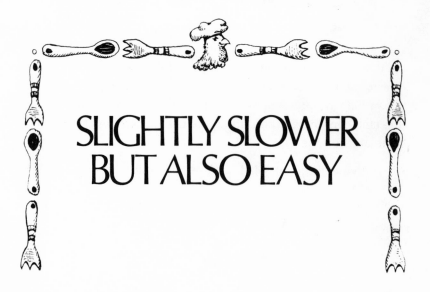

SLIGHTLY SLOWER BUT ALSO EASY

These are all simple recipes that you can prepare after school. Some of them, like Veal Wizardry and Chicken Tomato Casserole, require almost no preparation time but several hours in the oven. Others, like Protein Pizza and Anne's Pork Chops, require some—but not much—preparation time.

$ **PROTEIN PIZZA**

The easiest way to get a pizza on the table is to buy one fresh-made or frozen. If you want to serve a protein-rich main-dish pizza, however, you had better make it yourself.

1 tbsp (15 ml) margarine
2 onions, sliced into rings
½ green pepper, sliced into strips
1 lb. (.45 kg) ground beef
8-oz. (224 g) container refrigerator crescent rolls
8-oz. (224 g) can tomato sauce
½ tsp (2½ ml) oregano

1 tsp (5 ml) salt
5-oz. (140 g) can sliced mushrooms, drained
4-oz. (112 g) package mozzarella cheese, thinly sliced
¼ cup (60 ml) grated Parmesan cheese

1.   Melt margarine in a large skillet and sauté onions and peppers until limp but not brown. Remove to a plate, using a slotted
spoon.
2.   Break the ground beef into small pieces in the skillet and
fry until all of the meat has turned brown.
3.   In the meantime, lay the crescent rolls out on a greased
cookie sheet. The rolls have been perforated, but don't pull
them apart. Instead pat the perforations together so that the
dough is in one solid piece. Then pat it out toward the edges to
cover an oblong surface 9 by 14 inches (22.5 by 35 cm). Turn up
the edges of the dough to provide ½-inch (1.25 cm) sides. NOTE:
You are making an oblong, not a round, pizza.
4.   Spoon the tomato sauce evenly over the dough and sprinkle
with oregano and salt.
5.   Lift the ground beef out of the skillet with a slotted spoon,
draining off any extra fat. Scatter the beef evenly over the sauce.
6.   Place the onions, peppers, and mushrooms on top of the

beef. You can do this in a pattern or you can scatter them all over the pizza.

7.   Lay the mozzarella cheese slices on top of the vegetables in a single layer and sprinkle with Parmesan cheese.

8.   Bake in a preheated 400°F (200°C) oven until the crust is golden brown, about 25 minutes. Cut into squares.

Serve with a tossed salad and rice pudding. If yours is a family of big eaters, serve a hearty soup as a first course.

---

o   **VEAL WIZARDRY**

1½ to 2 lbs. (.68 to .90 kg) boneless veal stewing meat
4 large carrots cut in quarters crosswise
Few grinds pepper
1 can condensed cream of mushroom soup
1 envelope (4-serving size) dry onion soup mix

1.   Put all of the ingredients in a large casserole.

2.   Bake covered in 350°F (175°C) oven for 2 hours.

Serve with baked potatoes or brown rice, broccoli, and gingerbread with applesauce.

---

o   **SIMPLE PORK CHOPS**

---

4 shoulder pork chops
1 can condensed cream of chicken or mushroom soup
½ cup (120 ml) milk

1.   Trim some of the fat from the pork chops. Fry the fat in a hot skillet until about 1 tbsp of liquid fat has accumulated.

2.   Remove the pieces of fat, add the pork chops, and brown well on both sides.

[24]

3. Add the soup and milk. Cover and simmer slowly for 45 minutes.

Serve with mashed potatoes, peas, cider salad, and chocolate ice cream.

ANNE'S PORK CHOPS

---

4 large, thick pork chops or 8 thin pork chops
2 cups (480 ml) bread crumbs
⅓ cup (80 ml) thinly sliced celery
⅓ cup (80 ml) chopped onion
⅓ cup (80 ml) chopped green pepper (optional)
½ tsp (2.5 ml) oregano
¼ tsp (1 ml) sage
½ tsp (2.5 ml) dried parsley
1 egg
Tomato juice

1. Place 4 pork chops in a lightly greased casserole or baking dish large enough so that they may lie flat or overlap only slightly.
2. Put all of the other ingredients except the egg and the tomato juice in a bowl. Beat the egg into ⅓ (80 ml) cup tomato juice and pour over the dry mixture in the bowl. Stir together well. The crumbs should be moist but not mushy. If necessary add a little more tomato juice.
3. Spoon the bread crumb mixture over the chops. If you are using thin chops, place the remaining four chops on top of the crumb mixture.
4. Pour ⅔ cup (160 ml) tomato juice around the edge of the baking dish. Bake uncovered in a preheated 350°F (175°C) oven for 1 hour.

Serve with baked squash, Waldorf salad, and custard.

1 lb. (.45 kg) sausage meat
1 medium-sized onion, chopped
¼ cup (60 ml) chopped green pepper
1 cup (240 ml) raw rice
2 cups (480 ml) liquid—consommé, bouillon, tomato juice,
    or combine condensed mushroom soup and water
1 tsp (5 ml) salt

1.   Crumble sausage in a skillet and brown well. Pour off fat.
2.   Add other ingredients and pour into a well-greased casserole with a tight-fitting cover, or cover tightly with foil.
3.   Bake 1 hour in a 400°F (200°C) oven, checking at least once and adding water if the mixture looks dry. You may cook this in a skillet on top of the stove, if you prefer, but be careful that it does not dry out and stick to the bottom of the skillet.

Serve with peas, raw carrots, and peaches with ice cream and raspberry sauce.

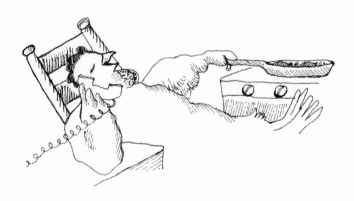

BASIC OVEN-FRIED CHICKEN

Traditional fried chicken demands a lot of fat and a lot of attention. I prefer this crispy but carefree recipe.

2½- to 3-lb. (1.10- to 1.35-kg) broiler-fryer, cut up, or 2 to
   3 pounds (.90 to 1.35 kg) chicken pieces
⅓ cup (80 ml) margarine
Flour, cracker crumbs, corn flake crumbs, or cornmeal
½ tsp (2.5 ml) salt (omit salt if you use salted cracker crumbs)
Few grinds pepper
2 tbsp (30 ml) instant flour (optional)
½ cup (120 ml) milk (optional)
1 cup (240 ml) broth or bouillon (optional)

1.   Rinse chicken pieces in cold water and dry on paper towels. (Optional: If you are using a whole chicken, put the back, wingtips, neck, and giblets in a small saucepan. Cover with water and simmer 1 hour. Strain the broth, and chop the giblets to be used in the gravy.)
2.   Grease a large flat baking dish. Be lavish, using at least 1 tbsp (15 ml) of the margarine. Melt the rest of the margarine separately.
3.   Dip each dried piece of chicken in the melted margarine and then in the flour or crumbs. Place the chicken pieces in the baking pan in a single layer. They should be close together but not touching. Drizzle any remaining margarine over the pieces.
4.   Sprinkle with salt and pepper.
5.   Bake uncovered in a preheated 350°F (175°C) oven for 1 hour.
6.   If you choose to make gravy, remove the chicken to a platter and scrape all of the brown crusty material left in the pan into a small saucepan. Stir the flour into the milk and add to the crusty material. Add broth (either with giblets as prepared by you or use canned broth or a chicken bouillon cube dissolved in boiling water). Bring to a boil to thicken. If the gravy is too thick, add more milk or broth.

Low-fat Chicken. Dry the chicken but do not coat it with crumbs or flour. Butter the baking dish lightly. Arrange the pieces in the pan and sprinkle with salt and pepper. Squeeze juice of ½ lemon over chicken if you like. Bake 1 hour. If the chicken looks pale when it is finished baking, run it under the broiler until lightly browned.

Chicken Parmesan. Dip the chicken in a mixture of ⅛ tsp (.5 ml) garlic powder, ¾ cup (180 ml) bread crumbs, ¼ cup (60 ml) Parmesan cheese. Bake according to basic directions. This is equally good served cold.

Serve with mashed potatoes, asparagus, sunshine salad, and butterscotch pudding.
or
Serve cold with potato salad, green beans, sliced tomatoes, and fruit pie or cobbler.

$ **EGG FOO CASSEROLE**

---

6 eggs
1 16-oz. (448 g) can bean sprouts, drained and rinsed under cold water
1 cup (240 ml) cooked rice
1 cup (240 ml) thinly sliced celery
¼ cup (60 ml) sliced green onions (or finely chopped white onions)
½ cup (120 ml) milk
½ tsp (2.5 ml) salt
Soy sauce
1 tbsp (15 ml) cornstarch
1 cup (240 ml) chicken broth

1. Beat eggs in a large bowl and add bean sprouts, rice, celery, onions, milk, salt, and 1 tbsp soy sauce.
2. Pour into a well-greased flat casserole—10-inch (25 cm) square or 12- by 7½-inch (30 by 19 cm) oblong. Bake in 350°F (175°C) oven until the mixture is puffed and lightly browned, about 35 minutes. Cut into squares.
3. In the meantime, prepare a sauce by mixing the cornstarch with a little of the chicken broth. Put in a small saucepan with the rest of the chicken broth and another 1 tbsp (15 ml) soy sauce. Cook over medium heat, stirring constantly, until the mixture thickens slightly. Serve sauce over the egg mixture.

Serve with frozen Oriental vegetables or green peas, whole wheat toast or health muffins, and apples and candy bars.

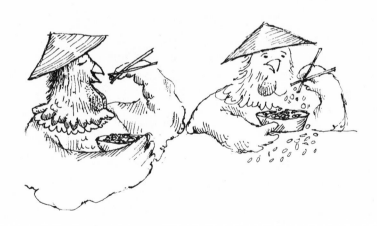

LEMON FLOUNDER BAKE

1 cup (240 ml) raw rice
¼ cup (60 ml) chopped onion
2 tbsp (30 ml) butter or margarine
2 tbsp (30 ml) flour
1 cup (240 ml) milk or light cream
¼ cup (60 ml) lemon juice
Peel of ½ lemon, grated
1½ to 2 lbs. (.68 to .90 kg) flounder fillets (thawed, if frozen)
Seasoned salt

1.   Cook rice according to package directions.
2.   Meanwhile, sauté onion in butter until limp. Add flour, and allow to bubble briefly. Stir in milk and continue stirring over low heat until sauce is thick and smooth. Then add lemon juice and grated lemon peel.
3.   Spoon the hot rice into a greased baking dish.
4.   Sprinkle the fish with seasoned salt and roll each piece tightly. Place rolls, seam side down, on rice.
5.   Pour sauce over the rolls and bake in a 400°F (200°C) oven for 20 minutes or until the fish flakes easily.

Serve with broccoli, beet pickles, and ice cream pie.

O $ ## EVERYBODY'S TUNA CASSEROLE

2 cups (480 ml) macaroni—or noodles, or spaghetti broken into 2-inch (5 cm) pieces
1 can cream of mushroom soup
¼ cup (60 ml) milk
7-oz. (196 g) can tuna
Slices of American cheese

1.   Cook the macaroni according to package directions. Drain and return to the pan in which it was boiled.
2.   Stir the soup, milk, and tuna into the macaroni.
3.   Spoon the macaroni mixture into a buttered casserole and top with a single layer of American cheese slices.
4.   Bake in a 350°F oven (175°C) oven until the cheese is melted and the mixture is bubbly, about 20 minutes.

To vary, add any of the following to the tuna mixture: ¼ cup (60 ml) finely chopped onion, ¼ cup (60 ml) finely chopped green pepper, 1 to 2 cups (240 to 480 ml) cooked peas or peas and carrots, 1 or 2 sliced hard-cooked eggs. Instead of cheese, top with crushed potato chips, corn flakes, or bread crumbs. Dot bread crumbs with butter.

Serve with lettuce wedges, sliced tomatoes, whole wheat bread, and a fruit compote topped with sherbet.

CHICKEN-TOMATO CASSEROLE

2 tbsp (30 ml) oil
2 medium-sized onions, sliced
2 tbsp (30 ml) flour
2 lbs. (.90 kg) chicken thighs
1 tsp (5 ml) salt
Few grinds pepper
2 tsp (10 ml) brown sugar
8-oz. (224 g) can tomato sauce

1.   Put oil in the bottom of a deep casserole or Dutch oven. Lay the onion slices on top of the oil and sprinkle with flour. Lay the chicken thighs on top of the onions.

2.   Sprinkle salt, pepper, and brown sugar over the chicken. Pour tomato sauce on top.

3.   Cover the casserole with a tight-fitting lid or foil. Bake in preheated 350°F (175°C) oven for 2 hours.

Serve with baked potatoes, corn, cabbage slaw, and coffee ice cream.

Thrifty tuna or clam sandwiches can be transformed into an elegant puff. The bread should soak in the milk-and-egg mixture for at least 2 hours before baking.

> 8-oz. (224 g) can minced clams or 7-oz. (196 g) can tuna
> ¼ cup (60 ml) thinly chopped celery
> ¼ cup (60 ml) chopped onion
> ¼ cup (60 ml) chopped green pepper
> ¼ cup (60 ml) mayonnaise
> Few grinds pepper
> 8 slices firm white bread—at least several days old
> 3 eggs
> 2 cups (480 ml) liquid. With clams use juice from clams, and enough whole milk to make 2 cups (480 ml); with tuna use all skim or whole milk.
> ½ cup (120 ml) grated Cheddar, Swiss, or American cheese

1. Drain minced clams into a measuring cup, or drain and discard any liquid on the tuna. Break tuna into small pieces with a fork. Combine the clams or the tuna with the celery, onion, green pepper, and mayonnaise.
2. Grease a 9-inch (225 cm) square baking pan and lay 4 slices of bread flat in the bottom of the pan. Top each slice of bread with a quarter of the clam or tuna mixture. Spread mixture out to the edges of the bread slices. Top with the other four slices of bread to form four sandwiches.
3. Beat together the eggs and liquid. Pour over the sandwiches. If the top slices of bread float, anchor them with a toothpick in the center of each. Refrigerate for 2 to 12 hours.
4. Preheat oven to 400°F (200°C). Remove any toothpicks. Sprinkle the cheese on top of the sandwiches. Bake until puffy and brown, about 40 minutes. Serve immediately.

Serve with beets, slaw with peanuts, and fruit crisp.

[33]

ROASTS–TODAY AND TOMORROW

Roast beef, ham, turkey, roast pork. Most people think of these as company meals. The fact is, they are all super-simple. All you need to know is how to turn on the oven and how to tell time to produce a "special occasion" meal.

The secret of a good roast is in the shopping. Since you don't really do anything to the meat except cook it, it must be good to begin with. If you are an inexperienced shopper, ask the person behind the meat counter for help. Also look for specials as good roasts can be expensive.

In most cases, you can count on leftovers. This chapter tells how to cook a roast originally and then how to jazz up the leftovers.

O   **ROAST BEEF**

2½ to 3 lbs. (1.10 to 1.35 kg) *boneless* roast beef.
Select eye round, top round, silver tip, sirloin, or rump.

1.   If convenient, leave the roast out of the refrigerator for a

few hours so that it will be at room temperature. If not, add a few minutes to the roasting time.

2. Preheat the oven to 500°F (260°C). Put a meat thermometer into the center of the roast and place the roast, fat side up, on a rack in a shallow pan. Place the roast in the oven, close the oven door, and turn the temperature down to 325°F (160°C).

3. The meat will be rare—pink but not bloody—in about 1½ hours. The thermometer should register 140°F (60°C). Well-done beef, 180°F (80°C) will take about 2 hours.

4. Don't worry if the beef is done before the rest of the meal, but be sure to take it out of the oven. It will hold its heat and will be easier to slice if it has had a chance to stand at room temperature for about 15 minutes. Remove any strings that may be around the roast and cut the meat in thin slices running parallel to the string lines. Another way to determine how to slice the roast is to put the fatty side up and slice down through the fat. (See illustration.)

Serve with baked potatoes (put them in the oven 15 minutes after you have put the roast in), creamed cauliflower and peas, tossed salad, and sherbet. If you are out to impress, you might also add hot rolls and a first course—melon wedges or small bowls of jellied consommé.

O   ROAST FRESH PORK

Pork shoulder, loin, or fresh ham—about 3 pounds (1.35 kg) boneless, or 5 pounds (2.25 kg) with bone
Apple cider or apple juice (optional)

1.   Put meat fat side up on a rack in an open pan and place into a 350°F (175°C) oven. Allow about 40 minutes per pound.
2.   If you like, you may spoon a little cider, about 2 tbsp (30 ml), over the roast from time to time. Some people think that this helps to "wash away" the pork fat.
3.   The most important thing to remember about fresh pork is that it must be cooked thoroughly—to an internal temperature of 185°F (85°C), or until the meat is white with no traces of pink. Undercooked pork could carry a sometimes fatal disease called trichinosis, which is destroyed by high temperature. Well-done pork is completely safe. Cook a 3-lb. (1.35 kg) roast at least 2 hours; a 5-lb. (2.25 kg) roast about 3½ hours.

Serve with sweet potatoes, brussels sprouts, Waldorf salad, and brownies.

O   ROLLED OR CANNED HAM

2 to 3 lbs. (.90 to 1.35 kg) rolled or canned ham
1 cup (240 ml) brown sugar
1 tsp (5 ml) dry mustard
½ cup (120 ml) cider, pineapple, apple, or orange juice

1.   Place ham on a rack in an open pan.
2.   Mix the sugar, mustard, and liquid together and spoon a little of this mixture over the ham.
3.   Bake in a 350°F (175°C) oven for 1 hour, basting with the brown-sugar mixture from time to time.

Serve with creamed potatoes and peas, fruit salad on greens, and Lazy Daisy cake.

---

o   **TURKEY ROASTS**

There was a time when turkey was only for Thanksgiving and Christmas. No longer! Two turkey roasts of special interest to people in a hurry are frozen boneless roasts and frozen prestuffed, prebasted whole birds. You can buy boneless roasts made of all white meat, a combination of white and dark, or all dark meat—in almost any size you require. Cook according to the instructions on the package. You can prepare packaged top-of-the-stove stuffing to go with it. The prestuffed whole birds I have prepared have been delicious. The stuffing has been tasty, and the meat has been juicy. And easy! You just take the frozen bird out of its plastic wrapper, cover it with foil, and put it in the oven. Instructions come with the birds.

Serve turkey and dressing with cranberry sauce, baked squash, green salad, and mince pie.

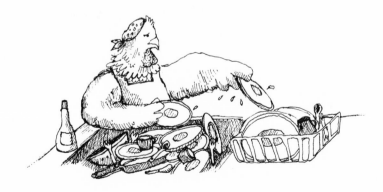

Leftovers

The obvious thing to do with leftover roast is to slice it very thinly for sandwiches. Sometimes, especially in the summer, a good thick sandwich, a salad, and a cup of soup is all that is required for dinner.

More suitable-for-supper leftover dishes are suggested in this section. All of them are very fast, easy, hearty, and tasty.

o   HOT SANDWICHES

If you have leftover gravy to match your leftover roast, you are in luck. If not, buy a can of gravy or make it from a mix. Heat the gravy while you mix up the appropriate number of servings of instant mashed potatoes. Put slices of leftover roast beef, pork, or poultry into the gravy just long enough to heat, about 5 minutes. Toast a slice of bread for each member of the family. Put the toast and a mound of potatoes on each plate. Lift the meat out of the gravy and layer it on the toast. Spoon the gravy over the meat and the potatoes. A few hot french fried onion rings, frozen or canned, add a festive touch to the plate.

Serve with lima beans, fruit salad, and cupcakes.

SCALLOPED POTATOES AND . . .

Stir a cup or two (240 to 480 ml) of ham or pork pieces into scalloped potatoes made from the recipe on page 81 or from a packaged mix.

Serve with broccoli, tomatoes, carrot and celery sticks, and fruit and cookies.

CREAMED SOUP AND . . .

Add a cup or two (240 to 480 ml) of meat, poultry, or fish pieces to a can of cream of mushroom, chicken, celery, or cheese soup. Also add sautéed mushrooms, onions, or cooked peas. Heat thoroughly. If the mixture looks drab, add a chopped pimiento or sprinkle with paprika or parsley.

Serve over rice with beets, cabbage slaw, and apple pie.

TOSSED SALAD AND . . .

Add strips of almost any leftover meat or combinations of meats along with any leftover *unsauced* vegetables to a tossed green salad. You may also add strips of cheese, slices of hard-cooked egg, and tomato wedges. Toss with an oil-and-vinegar dressing.

Serve with muffins, rolls, or biscuits, and blueberry pie with ice cream. If the salad seems a bit skimpy, serve a hearty soup as a first course.

CREATIVE CONCOCTIONS TO SERVE AND STORE

It's a miserable rainy Saturday afternoon. All your friends are busy. You've read the books you brought home from the library. You could watch an old movie on television. Or you could go to the kitchen and create a masterpiece—one that will delight your family tonight and also stand ready in the freezer for your next turn to cook.

This chapter contains recipes for four basic dishes—spaghetti sauce, meat loaf, beef or lamb stew, and stewed chicken —but each may be prepared with a variety of ingredients and seasonings that will make them distinctly yours. Then when someone says, "Great! Where did you get the recipe?" you can modestly claim it as your own.

Whichever of the four you choose to make, you will have enough to serve your family on two or more occasions. All freeze well and can be served in several guises.

When preparing a dish for the freezer, be sure that it is cooled quickly and wrapped tightly. You'll need one or more freezer-to-oven casseroles. You can line such a casserole with foil before you fill it. When the food is frozen solid remove it in the foil from the casserole. Wrap it well and return it to the freezer. The casserole dish is then freed for other uses. When you are ready to heat the frozen food, simply place it, still wrapped in the foil, back in the casserole. Saves washing a dish, too! Generally speaking, it is wise to plan to serve a frozen main dish within a few weeks.

$ **YOUR VERY OWN SOON-TO-BE- FAMOUS SPAGHETTI SAUCE**

Supermarket shelves contain many brands of spaghetti sauce but none of them is as good and as inexpensive as the sauce you make yourself. Unlike traditional sauces that require three or more hours of simmering, this sauce can be made in less than an hour. You can season it as you like. It will provide twelve or more servings, to eat now and freeze for later use. Several suggestions for serving it follow the recipe for the basic sauce.

1 tsp (5 ml) salt
2 to 3 lbs. (.95 to 1.35 kg) chopped beef (or 2 lbs. [.95 kg] beef and 1 package hamburger extender)
1 cup (240 ml) chopped onion
1 cup (240 ml) finely chopped carrots, celery, or green pepper, or a combination of any two or all three (optional)
3 cans condensed tomato soup, about 30 oz. (840 g)
1 15-oz. (420 g) can tomato sauce
½ cup (120 ml) water

Your choice of any or all of the following seasonings:
Garlic—squeezed from 1 clove or ½ tsp (2.5 ml) garlic powder
1 tbsp (15 ml) instant coffee
1 bay leaf, crumbled
Basil—1 pinch to 2 tsp (10 ml)
Oregano—start with 1 tsp (5 ml) and add more later
Worcestershire sauce—start with 1 tbsp (15 ml)

[41]

Hot pepper sauce—start with a few drops
Chili powder—start with ½ tsp (2.5 ml)
Black pepper—start with a few grinds

1.   Begin with a large, deep skillet, Dutch oven, or sauce pot. It must hold at least 3 quarts (2.85 l). (If you have any doubts, measure the pot by pouring 3 quarts [2.85 l] of water into it before you begin. Be sure to empty the pot and dry it well before you start the sauce.) Sprinkle the salt evenly over the bottom of the pot and place over moderate heat. Heat the salt for 1 minute. Then add the beef (and the hamburger extender mixed according to package directions). Break up the beef and keep it moving until it begins to give off its own fat. Add the onion (and the other chopped vegetables). Stir until all of the meat has turned brown.

2.   Add the soup, sauce, water, and your choice of seasonings. Taste as you add. Remember: Once you put a flavoring into the pot, you can't take it out. Go easy at first.

3.   When the sauce begins to boil, turn down the heat so that it continues to simmer but doesn't splatter all over the stove. Simmer uncovered for about 25 minutes, stirring frequently and adding more water if the sauce should become too thick. Turn off the heat.

4.   Stir the sauce to distribute the meat evenly. Pour the sauce to be frozen for future meals into appropriate containers. Remember that the sauce will expand as it freezes so be sure to leave at least 1 inch of space at the top of each container. When the sauce has cooled for at least an hour, cover it tightly and mark the lid with a waterproof pen. On the day that you wish to use the frozen sauce, put the container into a pan of hot water about an hour before you plan to use it. It should then thaw enough so that you can empty the sauce into a pan. Put the pan over very low heat. Add a little water or tomato juice if the sauce seems too thick. Also add another pinch of oregano.

5.   Serve the sauce—either fresh-made or from the freezer—in one of the recipes below.

O $ **OLD-FASHIONED ITALIAN SPAGHETTI**

Sauce, about 1 quart (.95 l)
½ tsp (2.5 ml) oregano
Spaghetti or other pasta—allow about 2½ oz. (70 g) of uncooked pasta for each big eater. Cook according to package directions.
Grated Italian cheese.

1.   Heat the sauce with oregano.
2.   Serve over the pasta. Pass the cheese to be sprinkled on top
of the sauce.

Serve with a vegetable-rich tossed salad and fresh or canned
fruit and cookies.

Sauce, about 2 cups (480 ml)
Frozen cheese-filled ravioli without sauce, about 16 oz.
2 tbsp Italian cheese
¼ cup bread crumbs

1.   Spoon a thin coating of the sauce into the bottom of a buttered shallow casserole. Place the ravioli close together or overlapping on top of the sauce. Spoon more sauce over the ravioli to cover them well.

2.   Combine the cheese and bread crumbs and sprinkle over the sauce.

3.   Bake in a preheated 350°F (175°C) oven until the mixture is bubbly and the crumbs begin to brown. This should take about 30 minutes.

Serve with French or Italian bread, a tossed vegetable salad, and sherbet.

$ **"MORE"**

2 cups (480 ml) raw macaroni or small shells cooked according to package directions

2½ cups (600 ml) sauce

2 cups (480 ml) cooked vegetables—carrots, peas, beans, limas, corn, or mixed. They may be leftovers, canned, or cooked frozen vegetables.

6 black olives, sliced (optional)

4 American cheese slices cut in quarters

1.   Combine all of the ingredients except the cheese and spoon into a buttered casserole. Top with cheese. Cover with a lid or foil and bake 20 minutes in a preheated 350°F (175°C) oven. Uncover and bake another 10 minutes.

"More" freezes well—don't add the cheese until you take it from the freezer—so you may want to prepare one or more of these casseroles on the day you make the sauce. When baking a casserole from the frozen state, put into a cold oven, turn oven to 350°F (175°C), and bake one hour. Uncover, add cheese, and bake another 10 minutes. "More" is practically indestructible and can sit around in the oven for a long time. Just recover it once it reaches the bubbly-brown state and turn the heat as low as possible.

Serve with lettuce wedges and Thousand Island dressing and a fruit cobbler.

Note: Small quantities of leftover sauce are delicious stirred into cooked green beans, corn, or zucchini. If you are left with not quite enough sauce for one of the preceding recipes, stretch what you have with canned tomato sauce or tomato soup.

$ TRIPLE-DUTY MIX

The following basic meat loaf recipe serves twelve. You may make it into two large loaves, baking one now and freezing the other. Each will serve four and provide leftovers for sandwiches.

You may also divide the mix into three equal portions to be served as meat loaf, ground beef a la mode, or Danish meatballs.

> 2 eggs
> Liquid: 1 cup (240 ml) milk, evaporated milk, or tomato juice; or 1 can condensed cream of mushroom soup or cream of tomato soup
> 3 lbs. (1.35 kg) ground beef
> 1½ cups (360 ml) filler—oatmeal, bread crumbs, wheat germ, or a combination
> 1 medium-sized onion, chopped
> 1 tsp (5 ml) salt
> Few grinds pepper
> 1 tbsp (15 ml) Worcestershire sauce
> ½ tsp (2.5 ml) of any of the following seasonings: garlic powder, savory, thyme, or mixed herbs

1. Beat the eggs lightly in a large mixing bowl and add all of the other ingredients. Mix lightly. Use your hands to do the job quickly.

MEAT LOAF

1. Divide the mix between two or three loaf pans or put one third in a loaf pan and use the rest in the recipes below.
2. Preheat oven to 350°F (175°C) and bake loaf 1 hour. Remove from oven and let sit 10 minutes. Pour off juices and lift loaf from the pan with a pancake turner.

Or cover the loaf pan with foil and wrap well in a plastic bag. Freeze. You may unwrap, defrost, and bake 1 hour at 350°F (175°C) or you may unwrap and put the frozen loaf in a cold oven. Turn oven to 350°F (175°C) and bake for 2 hours.

Serve with scalloped potatoes, limas, fruit salad, and spice cake.

COLD MEAT LOAF

Sometimes it makes sense to bake two loaves at one time. Refrigerate one of the loaves for a day or two.

Serve sliced cold meat loaf with chili sauce, potato salad, zucchini, and blueberry pie.

GROUND BEEF A LA MODE

⅓ of triple-duty mix
4 servings instant mashed potatoes prepared according to package directions
1 tbsp (15 ml) butter or margarine
2 tbsp (30 ml) instant flour
Water
Bottled gravy coloring

1.   Spoon the mix into a 9-inch (22.5 cm) pie plate, packing it against the bottom and sides of the pan with the back of the spoon. Bake in 350°F (175°C) oven for 30 minutes (or wrap tightly and freeze to be *thawed* and baked later).
2.   After baking for 30 minutes, the meat will have pulled away from the pan and juices will have accumulated. Pour the juices into a small saucepan.

3.   Spoon the mashed potatoes on the meat to completely cover it. Dot with butter. Return to the oven for another 20 minutes.

4.   In the meantime, stir the flour into ⅓ cup (80 ml) cold water. Add to the meat juices and bring to a boil. Add more water if the gravy is too thick. Add enough gravy coloring to make it a rich brown.

5.   Cut meat and potato pie into wedges and serve with the gravy.

Serve with corn-on-the-cob or buttered frozen corn, spinach salad, and brownies.

DANISH MEATBALLS

⅓ of triple-duty mix
1 tbsp (15 ml) oil
Flour
1 beef bouillon cube or 1 packet instant beef broth
Water
½ cup (120 ml) sour cream or plain yogurt

1.   Shape the mix into balls about the size of walnuts. Put on a pie plate and place in the freezer, uncovered. When frozen solidly, remove the balls from the plate. (They will come off easily if you rub a hot, wet sponge over the bottom of the pie plate.) Put the meatballs in a plastic bag. Close the bag tightly and store in the freezer until ready to use. Do not thaw before browning as frozen meatballs will retain their shape while thawed ones are apt to fall apart.

2.   Heat the oil in a large skillet. Dip the frozen meatballs into a small dish of flour to coat well on all sides. Brown in the oil, turning often.

3.   When all of the meatballs are well browned on all sides, add the bouillon and ¾ cup (180 ml) water. Simmer, covered, for

30 minutes. Mix 1 tbsp (15 ml) flour (use any that was left over from the dipping) with ¼ cup (60 ml) cold water. Add to the skillet. Bring to a boil. Add the sour cream or yogurt and heat until steamy but do not allow to boil again.

Serve with buttered noodles or brown rice, carrots with oregano, cabbage slaw, and strawberry sundaes.

BASIC BEEF OR LAMB STEW

The Hungarians call it goulash; the French call it Bourguignon; Americans call it stew. All have three basic ingredients—meat, vegetables, and gravy. Below is a basic recipe with variations. It will provide at least two meals for a family of four and can be frozen or held in the refrigerator for a day or two.

> Oil
> Approximately 3 lbs. (1.35 kg) of boneless beef chuck or boneless lamb cut into bite-sized cubes
> Flour
> 1 onion, chopped
> 1 clove garlic, minced (optional)

1½ cups (360 ml) liquid—bouillon, broth, vegetable juice, or
water
1 teaspoon salt
A few grinds pepper or a few drops of red hot pepper sauce
1 tbsp (15 ml) Worcestershire sauce
½ tsp (2.5 ml) dried herbs—oregano, thyme, rosemary, bay
leaf, or savory
Vegetables—fresh, canned, or frozen—carrots, celery,
onions, parsnips, turnips, mushrooms, peas, beans,
and/or limas
Instant flour
Water

1. Heat enough oil to cover the bottom of a large skillet
(with a tight-fitting cover) or a Dutch oven. Turn each piece of
meat in a small bowl of flour to coat evenly on all sides. Brown
the floured meat in the oil over moderately high heat, turning to
brown on all sides. Do not crowd the meat. Do several pieces
at a time, remove them to a plate when browned and add more
pieces of floured meat. Add more oil as necessary to keep the
meat from sticking.
2. When all of the meat has been browned and removed to
the plate, add the chopped onion and garlic to the skillet and
brown for 2 to 3 minutes. Pour off any excess oil.
3. Return the browned meat to the skillet with the liquid,
seasonings, and herbs. The liquid should almost—but not quite
—cover the meat. Cover and simmer over very low heat for 2
hours checking frequently to be sure there are at least several
cups of liquid on the meat.
4. Now for the vegetables. You can use as few or as many
different vegetables as you choose in almost any quantity. The
more vegetables you use, the more you can stretch the meat.
Three pounds of meat could easily be stretched to serve twelve
or more. Add raw vegetables 30 minutes before the meat is to
be finished cooking. Add frozen or canned vegetables at the
very end. When using canned vegetables, be sure to drain and
use the liquid as part of the liquid in which you cook the meat.

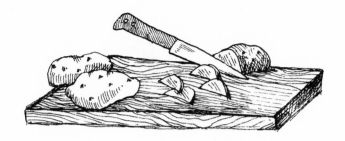

Here is an example of how to add the vegetables: After the meat has simmered for 1½ hours, add 1 cup (240 ml) sliced carrots, ½ cup (120 ml) sliced celery, and 8 very small white onions. Continue to simmer for 30 minutes or until the onions are tender when pierced with a fork. Then add a 10-oz. (280 g) package of frozen beans and simmer about 10 minutes until the beans are tender. Add a 4-oz. (112 g) can of mushroom pieces (having earlier drained the liquid from the can over the meat).

5. The sauce will be slightly thickened. If you wish to thicken it more, stir 2 tbsp (30 ml) of instant flour into ⅓ cup (80 ml) cold water. Pour into the simmering meat and vegetables and return to the boil.

6. Serve immediately, cool and reheat later, or freeze. Partially defrost frozen stew at room temperature and then pour into a well-buttered casserole to continue defrosting and baking in a 350°F (175°C) oven. You may wish to thin the frozen sauce with about ¼ cup (60 ml) broth or juice. NOTE: You may also freeze the stew before you add the vegetables or after you add the vegetables but before you thicken the gravy.

Serve stew with boiled potatoes, noodles, or rice, and lettuce wedges with Thousand Island dressing, and cherry pie.

You may cook the potatoes with the other raw vegetables in the stew but leave them whole or in halves and cook only enough for *one* meal. Potatoes do not reheat well.

SHEPHERD'S PIE

Stew for one meal, prepared according to basic directions
Prepared instant mashed potatoes—one serving per person
1 tbsp butter or margarine

1.   Place stew in a buttered casserole.
2.   Spoon mashed potatoes in a ring on top of the stew. Dot with butter.
3.   Place in a preheated 350°F (175°C) oven and bake until the stew is bubbly and the potatoes lightly browned—about 15 minutes if the stew goes into the oven hot, 30 minutes if it is cool when it goes in.

Serve with pickled beets and upside-down cake.

STEWED CHICKEN

Stewed or boiled chicken may not sound like the most appetizing meat in the world but it is the basis of some fantastic dishes. Following are basic instructions for stewing and then some suggestions for serving. Leftover cooked chicken or turkey and canned chicken broth may be substituted in any of the recipes that follow the basic recipe.

But first, a word about the main ingredient. Stewing chickens, or hens, or fowl—they go by different names in different parts of the country—are old, fat, and flavorful. They usually weigh 5 to 6 lbs. (2.25 to 2.70 kg) and require a long cooking time. Fryers, weighing about 3 lbs. (1.35 kg) and roasters weighing 4 to 5 lbs. (1.80 to 2.25 kg) may also be stewed. They require a much shorter cooking time.

$ BASIC RECIPE

> 5 to 6 lbs. (2.25 to 2.70 kg) chicken—either 1 fowl or 2 smaller birds—whole or cut into pieces
> 1 rib of celery with leafy top
> 1 carrot, cut in quarters crosswise
> 1 onion, halved
> 1 tsp (5 ml) salt
> Water

1.   Put the chicken, vegetables, and salt into a large pot and add water to come within a few inches of the top of chicken, about 1 quart (.95 l).

2.   Simmer very slowly, covered, until the meat begins to fall off of the leg bones and the breast meat feels tender when pierced with a fork—about 45 minutes for young birds, 2 to 3 hours for a stewing chicken.

3.   Turn off the heat and lift the bird into a colander to drain, or pour into a strainer over a bowl large enough to hold all of the broth. Set aside until cool enough to handle. Remove skin and discard or use in preparing rich broth. Remove all of the meat from the bones, taking care to keep large pieces intact.

4.   If you have time and want a lot of really rich broth, return the bones, skin, and vegetables to the broth in the large pot. Add another 2 cups (480 ml) of water. Continue to simmer, covered, for another 2 hours. Strain the broth into a large bowl, discarding everything that remains in the strainer.

Note: To freeze, put the chicken pieces in plastic containers and cover with broth. Allow room for expansion. Freeze remaining broth in a separate container.

$ **FIRST-DAY STEWED CHICKEN**

1½ cups (360 ml) broth—see recipe above
¼ cup (60 ml) instant flour
½ cup (120 ml) milk or cream
¼ tsp (1 ml) nutmeg
Large slices of chicken stewed according to the recipe above
   (the number your family will eat at one sitting)

1.   Put the broth in the top of a double boiler. Stir the flour into the milk and add to the broth. Bring to a boil over direct heat.

2.   Add the slices of chicken and sprinkle with nutmeg.

3.   Put the chicken and gravy in the top of the double boiler over boiling water in the bottom of the double boiler and heat.

Or, you may put the chicken pieces in a flat buttered casserole and pour the gravy over it. Sprinkle with nutmeg. Bake in a 325°F (160°C) oven until bubbly, about 15 minutes.

Serve with mashed potatoes or rice, broccoli, cranberry sauce, and peppermint ice cream.

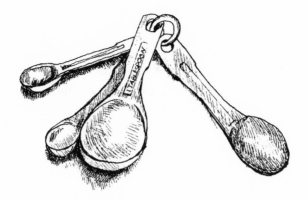

$

CHICKEN-RICE SALAD

½ cup (120 ml) uncooked rice
1 cup (240 ml) chicken broth or bouillon
3 cups (720 ml) cooked chicken cut into bite-sized pieces
2 hard-boiled eggs, sliced
¼ cup (60 ml) chopped green pepper
¼ cup (60 ml) chopped green onion
¼ cup (60 ml) chopped canned pimiento
¼ cup (60 ml) chopped celery
1 tsp salt
Few grinds pepper
¼ cup (60 ml) sour cream or mayonnaise
1 tbsp (15 ml) chili sauce
1 tbsp (15 ml) bottled French dressing

1.   Cook rice in broth according to package directions.
2.   Combine the rice with all of the other ingredients. Taste for seasoning. Add more sour cream for a moister salad.
3.   Chill for several hours.

Serve on greens with sliced tomatoes and cucumbers, bread sticks or hard rolls, and strawberry shortcakes.

$ CHICKEN TETRAZZINI

2 cups (480 ml) spaghetti, broken into 2-inch (5 cm) pieces
Cooked chicken or turkey—large slices are best
4-oz. (112 g) can mushrooms, drained (save liquid)
¼ cup (60 ml) butter or margarine
1 small onion, chopped
2 tbsp (30 ml) flour
1½ cups (360 ml) chicken broth and mushroom liquid
1 tsp (5 ml) salt
Dash pepper
Dash nutmeg
⅓ cup (80 ml) sherry (optional)
3 tbsp (45 ml) cream
2 tbsp (60 ml) grated Parmesan cheese

1. Cook spaghetti according to package directions and drain. Place in a buttered shallow casserole. Lay chicken and then mushrooms on top of spaghetti.
2. In the meantime, make sauce. Melt butter in small pan and sauté onions until limp. Stir in flour and allow to bubble for a few seconds. Stir in broth, salt, pepper, and nutmeg. Stir until smooth and add sherry and cream. Pour over chicken and sprinkle with grated cheese.
3. Bake casserole in 400°F (200°C) oven until bubbly and lightly browned, about 20 minutes.

Serve with tossed vegetable salad, fruit, and cookies.

$ BAKED CHICKEN CROQUETTES

½ cup (120 ml) uncooked rice
1 cup (240 ml) broth
½ cup (120 ml) mayonnaise or salad dressing

1 tbsp (15 ml) chopped green pepper
1 tbsp (15 ml) chopped onion
1 tbsp (15 ml) chopped pimiento
½ tsp (2.5 ml) salt
Few grinds pepper
2 cups minced or ground cooked chicken or turkey
Cornmeal
Gravy or mushroom soup sauce

1.   Cook rice in broth according to package directions.
2.   Combine all of the ingredients, except the cornmeal and gravy and chill for several hours.
3.   Half an hour before dinner, remove from the refrigerator and shape with your hands into smooth balls or log shapes, using ½ cup (120 ml) of the mixture for each croquette. Roll in cornmeal and place in a heavily greased shallow baking dish.
4.   Bake in a preheated 450°F (230°C) oven for 20 to 25 minutes or until well browned. Spoon hot leftover or canned chicken gravy, or a hot mushroom sauce, made by thinning canned mushroom soup with milk, over the croquettes.

Serve with baked squash, spinach salad, and custard and cookies.

VITAL VEGETABLES

Vegetables are beautiful. If they served no other purpose, they would be used to brighten the plate. They are also packed with vitamins and are essential to good nutrition. Ordinary vegetables can be made to delight the palate with very little effort. You will be surprised to discover what a pinch of oregano can do for the carrot or what a sprinkling of nutmeg can do for spinach. The chart beginning on the following page lists seasonings and sauces to add sparkle to twenty vegetables, whether purchased raw, frozen, or canned.

The same chart tells how to buy and prepare fresh vegetables. Fresh carrots, celery, onions, and green peppers are available year round and are usually cheaper than either frozen or canned. Other vegetables are apt to be tasteless and expensive when they are purchased out of season. The general rule is to buy fresh vegetables when they are plentiful and cheap.

Canned vegetables are frequently more expensive and less attractive than frozen vegetables. (One exception is beets.) Heat—do not boil—canned vegetables in their own liquid.

Frozen vegetables are often the best buy and offer the greatest variety. Cook according to the directions on the package, being careful not to overcook.

	What to look for when selecting	How much to buy for each serving	How to prepare for cooking	Cook covered in small amount of boiling, salted water. Drain.
Asparagus	Uniform size and tight green tips	⅓–½ lb. (200g)	Wash under running water. Snap off and discard woody white ends. Peel off lower scales. Cut in halves crosswise.	Place stem ends in bottom of pan. Lay tips on top. 10 min.
Beans, Green or Wax	Small, bright, un-blemished. Push two ends of a bean toward one anoth-er. They should snap in two, not bend like rubber.	¼ lb. (115g)	Cut off tips. If small, leave whole. Cut or break larger beans into 2 or 3 pieces.	12 to 15 min.
Beets	Canned beets are usually less expensive and always quicker than fresh beets.			
Broccoli	Short stalks. Dark green—not yellow —tight flowers.	½ lb. (225g)	Soak 15 min. in cold salted water. Drain. Cut off yellow leaves and flowers. Split stalks vertically toward flower end. Cut very large stalks into 2 or 3 pieces.	12 min. or serve *flowers only* raw
Brussels Sprouts	Tight and un-blemished.	¼ lb. (115g)	Wash. Remove wilted leaves. Cut off stems and cut crosswise slits in stem ends of large sprouts.	10 to 20 min.
Cabbage, Green, White, or Red	Tight, smooth, and unblemished.	⅓ lb. (150g)	Wash. Remove brown or wilted leaves. Cut into wedges or shred on a coarse grater, or chop. For recipes using *raw* cabbage, see salad chapter.	7 to 12 min.
Carrots	Bright and un-blemished.	¼ lb. (115g)	Remove any green tops. Wash. Peel or scrape. Leave whole or cut into chunks, strips, or circles.	15 to 30 min. or serve *raw*

FROZEN	CANNED	SERVING SUGGESTIONS for frozen, canned, or fresh				
Cook according to package directions. Drain.	Heat to boiling point in liquid from can. Drain.	Butter, additional salt as required, and pepper	Cream sauce (see page 66)	Cheese sauce (see page 67)	Chill in oil-and-vinegar (see page 69)	Suggested additions
X	X	X	X		X	Nutmeg Lemon juice
X	X	X	X	X	X	Dill Thyme Fried bacon Sauteed almonds
X	X	X			X	Sour cream Orange juice
X		X	X	X		Marjoram Basil
X		X	X	X		Grated Italian cheese
		X	X	X		Caraway seeds Minced pimento
X	X	X	X			Oregano Brown sugar Maple syrup

	What to look for when selecting	How much to buy for each serving	How to prepare for cooking	Cook covered in small amount of boiling, salted water. Drain.
Cauliflower	Snow white and unblemished.	½ lb. (225g)	Remove all green leaves. Wash. Break or cut into flowerettes of uniform size.	10 to 15 min. or serve *raw*
Celery	Tight with fresh-looking leaves.	½ cup sliced (120ml)	Wash, remove leaves, and pull off strings. Slice thinly or in 1- to 3-inch pieces.	8 min. or serve *raw*
Corn	Freshness. It seldom pays to buy fresh corn out of season.	1 to 3 ears	Just before cooking remove husks and silks. Cut out any brown or wormy spots.	See special instructions below.
Lima Beans	Fresh lima beans are seldom available.			
Mushrooms	Whiteness. Cap should fit tightly around the stem exposing little of the black gills.	¼ lb. (115g)	Wipe each mushroom with a damp paper towel. Remove dark end of stem. Leave whole or cut into slices, quarters, or halves.	See special instructions below.
Onions	Firm and un-blemished.	¼ lb. (115g)	Remove flaky brown or white outer skin. Leave whole if small, or cut into quarters or slices.	10 to 40 min.
Parsnips	Small and relatively smooth.	¼ lb. (115g)	Wash and scrape or peel. Leave whole or cut in halves or quarters lengthwise.	20 to 40 min.
Peas	Fresh peas are delicious but expensive and time-consuming.			

FROZEN	CANNED			SERVING SUGGESTIONS for frozen, canned, or fresh			
Cook according to package directions. Drain.	Heat to boiling point in liquid from can. Drain.	Butter, additional salt as required, and pepper	Cream sauce (see page 66)	Cheese sauce (see page 67)	Chill in oil-and-vinegar (see page 69)	Suggested additions
X		X	X	X		Cooked peas
		X	X	X		Curry Nutmeg Peas Mushrooms
X	X	X	X		X	Chopped green pepper or onion Tomato sauce Lima beans
X	X		X		X	Dill Corn Tomato sauce
X	X		X		X	Tarragon Minced onions Garlic
X	X	X	X	X		Tomato sauce
		X				Nutmeg Brown sugar
X	X	X	X		X	Mint jelly Sage Marjoram

	What to look for when selecting	How much to buy for each serving	How to prepare for cooking	Cook covered in small amount of boiling, salted water. Drain.
Potatoes—see pages 78–83				
Spinach	Perky, dark-green leaves.	¼ lb. (115g)	Wash in cold water and then wash again. Discard yellow leaves, roots, and thick stems.	10 to 20 min. or serve *raw* in salads
Zucchini Squash	Small, smooth, and unblemished.	¼ lb. (115g)	Scrub with a brush. Do not peel. Cut into strips or rounds.	10 min. or serve *raw* if young and fresh
Acorn or Butternut Squash	Smooth skins with no soft spots.	1 sm. squash for 2	Wash. Cut in half and remove fibers and seeds.	See special instructions below.
Tomatoes	Bright, unblemished. Firm without being hard.		Rinse under cold water.	See special instructions below. Or serve *raw*
Turnips	Small white turnips with purple blushes or large yellow waxy rutabagas.	¼ lb. (115g)	Wash, peel, and cut into uniform-sized chunks.	15 to 30 min. or serve *raw*

SPECIAL INSTRUCTIONS:

Corn-on-the-Cob. Select a pot or deep skillet with a lid. It must be large enough to hold all of the corn. Half fill with water. Add 1 tsp. (5 ml) salt. Bring to the boil. Add the corn, one ear at a time, so that the water never stops boiling. Cover and cook 5 minutes. Use tongs to lift the ears from the water.

Mushrooms. To sauté 1 pound (448g), heat 3 tbsp. (45 ml) oil in a medium-sized skillet with a lid. Add the mushrooms and stir gently until they are coated with oil. Turn the heat to low, cover the skillet tightly, and steam for 5 minutes. Test for tenderness and steam another 2 or 3 minutes if necessary.

FROZEN	CANNED	SERVING SUGGESTIONS for frozen, canned, or fresh				
Cook according to package directions. Drain.	Heat to boiling point in liquid from can. Drain.	Butter, additional salt as required, and pepper	Cream sauce (see page 66)	Cheese sauce (see page 67)	Chill in oil-and-vinegar (see page 69)	Suggested additions
X	X	X	X	X		Nutmeg Hard-boiled egg Fried bacon
	X	X	X	X	X	Grated cheese Basil Oregano
X		X				Cinnamon Nutmeg Grated orange peel
	X					Oregano Bay leaf Basil Celery Onions
		X	X			Parsley

Acorn or Butternut Squash. Turn cut-side down in a baking pan large enough to hold the squash halves. Pour about ½-inch (1 cm) boiling water into the pan and bake in a preheated 350°F (175°C) oven for 20 minutes. Turn the squash cavity-side up. Sprinkle each cavity with salt, pepper, nutmeg, and brown sugar. Dot with butter or margarine. Return to the oven and continue to bake until tender, about 20 minutes. Leave in the shell to serve.

Tomatoes. To bake or broil medium-sized tomatoes, cut each one in half. Place cut-side up in a buttered baking dish. Sprinkle with salt, pepper, and bread or cracker crumbs. Dot with butter or margarine. Bake 20 minutes in a 350°F (175°C) oven or broil until the tops are browned, about 5 minutes. To cook cherry tomatoes, place whole in a buttered baking dish. Dot with butter and bake in 350°F (175°C) oven 5 to 10 minutes.

CREAMED VEGETABLES OLD STYLE

2 tbsp (30 ml) butter or margarine
2 tbsp (30 ml) flour
1 cup liquid (240 ml)—milk, cream, cooking liquid, broth, or a combination
2 to 3 cups (480 to 720 ml) cooked vegetables
Salt
Pepper

1. Melt butter in a heavy saucepan and stir in the flour. Allow to bubble for a few seconds.
2. Remove from the heat and stir in the liquid with a wire whisk.
3. Return to the heat until the sauce comes to a boil and thickens. Add the vegetables and seasoning.

"INSTANT" NONFAT CREAMED VEGETABLES

2 to 3 cups (480 to 720 ml) vegetables cooked in ¾ cup
(180 ml) water, or 2 to 3 cups canned vegetables, heated
in liquid
½ cup (120 ml) milk
2 tbsp (30 ml) instant flour
Salt
Pepper

1.   When the vegetables are tender, check to see that there
is about ½ cup (120 ml) liquid left in the saucepan with the
vegetables.
2.   Stir the flour into the milk and then stir into the vegetables
and liquid. Allow to bubble for a minute or two and taste for
seasoning. If the sauce is too thick, add a little more milk.

CHEESE SAUCE

Cream sauce prepared according to one of the recipes above
¼ to ¾ cups (60 to 180 ml) cubed or shredded American
or Cheddar cheese

1.   Add cheese to cream sauce and stir until melted and
smooth.

SPARKLING SALADS

There are many good things to say about salads. They are nutritious, delicious, and colorful. They can be prepared quickly. They offer scope to the imaginative cook because there is no limit to the ingredients and combinations that can be added to the salad bowl.

Follow these simple rules:

Raw vegetables must be fresh, clean, and dry.
Wash greens well; grit is the mortal enemy of all salads.
Dry greens in a strainer or with paper towels.

The salad dressing, which in most cases should be added at the last instant before serving, should enhance, not mask, the flavor of the basic salad ingredients. There are many good bottled dressings available in every grocery store. These are convenient but expensive compared to the dressings you can make yourself. Following are recipes for a basic oil-and-vinegar dressing, a no-fat sweet-and-sour dressing for green and vegetable salads, and a no-fat dressing for fruit salads. Other dressing ideas are included with the salad suggestions.

OIL-AND-VINEGAR DRESSING

2 tbsp (30 ml) oil—olive, vegetable, or corn
1 tbsp (15 ml) vinegar—wine, tarragon, or cider
1 tsp (5 ml) salt
½ tsp (2.5 ml) dry mustard
1 tsp (5 ml) sugar
Garlic salt (optional)
Hot red pepper sauce (optional)

Combine all of the ingredients in the bottom of your salad bowl or in a cup or small jar. (I mix them in the salad bowl and lay cucumbers, onions, or green peppers over the dressing. Soaking only improves them. Then I lay the greens on top of the cucumber-onion layer—well out of the dressing. I cover the bowl and refrigerate it, to be tossed at the last minute.)

If you prepare the dressing in a cup or jar, you will, of course, pour it over the salad at the last minute. If you are going to prepare it this way, you will probably want to double or triple the recipe and keep the dressing in the refrigerator for several future salads.

To vary add fresh or dried herbs. Substitute lemon juice for vinegar. Add finely chopped scallions or capers. If you want to make blue-cheese dressing, mash about 2 tbsp (30 ml) blue cheese and beat it into the dressing.

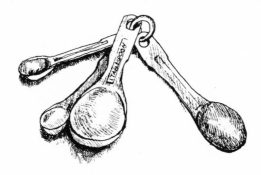

NO-FAT SWEET-AND-SOUR DRESSING

1 egg
1 cup (240 ml) sugar
½ cup (120 ml) vinegar—wine or cider
1 cup (240 ml) water
1 tsp (5 ml) salt
½ tsp (2.5 ml) dry mustard
A few drops hot pepper sauce

1.   Beat the egg in a small saucepan. Beat in the sugar and all of the other ingredients.
2.   Bring to a full boil over medium heat, stirring constantly. Boil 1 minute.
3.   Chill. Serve with green and vegetable salads. Particularly good with cabbage slaw or fresh spinach.

PINEAPPLE DRESSING

¼ cup (60 ml) sugar
2 tsp (10 ml) cornstarch
¼ tsp (1 ml) salt
¼ cup (60 ml) lemon or orange juice
½ cup (120 ml) pineapple juice
1 egg

1.   In a small saucepan combine the sugar, cornstarch, and salt. Add the juices. Place over very low heat, stirring constantly until the sauce begins to thicken.
2.   Beat the egg well, add a little of the hot mixture to the egg and then add the egg to the dressing.
3.   Cook just to the boiling point. Cool and refrigerate to be served with fruit salads.

TEN IDEAS FOR GREEN AND VEGETABLE SALADS

1. The vegetable chart beginning on page 60 lists 8 vegetables that are delicious when cooked and then chilled in the oil-and-vinegar dressing on page 69 or in bottled dressing. Since frozen or canned vegetables may be used, this is an especially good salad idea for winter months when fresh greens may be very expensive. Two other vegetables that should be added to the list are canned kidney beans and canned garbanza beans. Obviously canned vegetables do not require further cooking. Just drain off the liquid and coat the vegetables well with dressing. Cover and chill for several hours or overnight, turning the vegetables in the dressing several times. These chilled vegetables may be served alone, in combination, or may be tossed with greens and other fresh vegetables just before serving.

2.   The simplest salad is wedges of head lettuce. Try serving with a dressing made by combining mayonnaise and chili sauce in any proportions with or without a chopped-up hard-cooked egg. Or serve with bottled Russian or Thousand Island dressing.

3.   Add any or a combination of the following raw vegetables to a combination of greens: carrot, celery, cauliflower, broccoli flowers, green pepper, onions, turnips, radishes, tomatoes, or bean sprouts.

4.   Salads may be given a new look if you don't toss them. Instead, put greens on individual plates or bowls and top with slices of cucumber, "wheels" of green pepper, whole cherry tomatoes, flowerettes of cauliflowers, and so on. Pass a dressing. This is a particularly good idea if your main dish is a combination of several foods. For example, if you are serving a stew with beef, potatoes, carrots, and onions, a salad with 4 or 5 more ingredients all mixed together is not as attractive as one made up of several very distinct vegetables.

5.   Toss greens—fresh spinach is particularly good—with croutons in oil-and-vinegar dressing. Sprinkle with grated Parmesan cheese.

6.   Thinly slice one red onion and divide into rings. Add 1 well-drained 10-oz. (280 g) can mandarin oranges and about ½ cup (120 ml) oil-and-vinegar dressing. Toss with salad greens and 1 sliced avocado.

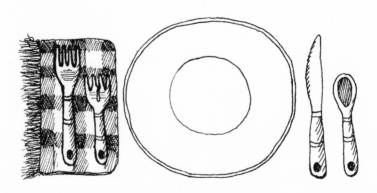

7.   Combine ¼ cup (60 ml) sliced radishes; ¼ cup (60 ml) sliced green onions; ½ cup (120 ml) sliced celery; and ¼ cup (60 ml) diced green peppers; 2 tomatoes, diced; and 1 8-oz. (224 g) carton cream-style cottage cheese. Season with freshly ground black pepper. Serve on salad greens or with avocado wedges.

8.   To make a good slaw, shred cabbage at least one hour before serving time. Moisten with no-fat, sweet-and-sour dressing mentioned at beginning of this chapter, or a combination of 1 tbsp vinegar, 1 tbsp sugar, salt, pepper, and sour cream. Chill.

9.   To vary slaw, add chopped onion, cucumber, carrot, and/or green pepper. Or add crumbled bacon, finely sliced olives, pickle relish, or caraway or poppy seeds.

10.   Moisten shredded cabbage with mayonnaise or sour cream and add chopped apple, pineapple chunks, chopped dates, chopped raisins, and/or walnuts, pecans, or salted peanuts.

SIX IDEAS FOR TOSSED FRUIT SALADS

Fruit salads with heavy dressings are delicious but are more suitable for desserts than to accompany meats. Here are suggestions for lighter salads.

Remember to drain canned or frozen fruits very well. Put in a sieve or colander over a bowl and refrigerate for several hours, making sure that the bottom of the sieve stays out of the syrup. The syrup that you drain off of the fruit may be substituted for up to half of the water to make a delicious gelatin. (See pages 76–77.)

1.   Waldorf salad is one of the all-time favorite fruit salads. Combine cubes or slices of apples (leave the skins on to add color) with chopped celery and nut meats. Sprinkle with lemon juice and moisten with mayonnaise or sour cream. Refrigerate to be served on lettuce. Pears may be substituted for apples.

Pineapple chunks, seedless grapes, raisins, or chopped dates may be added.

2.   Combine apples, celery, and seedless grapes with a dressing made by combining 2 tbsp (30 ml) milk, 2 tbsp (3ml) chunky peanut butter, and ½ cup (120 ml) mayonnaise.

3.   Slice bananas lengthwise and place on a bed of greens. Use the peanut butter dressing above. NOTE: Either peel the bananas at the last minute or coat them with lemon juice or fruit syrup to keep them from turning dark.

4.   Drain a 10-oz. (280 g) can mandarin oranges, a 13-oz. (360 g) can pineapple chunks, and an 8-oz. (224 g) can pear slices. Add raisins and a few coarsely chopped walnuts or pecans. Refrigerate in the sieve. Just before serving, toss with bite-sized greens and oil-and-vinegar or French dressing.

5.   Chop nuts, dates, and celery and moisten with mayonnaise. Mound this mixture on spiced peach halves or spiced apple slices on a bed of greens.

6.   Combine almost any canned, frozen, or fresh fruits in any proportion with the pineapple dressing given at the beginning of this chapter. Serve on greens.

Molded gelatin salads are a festive way to serve vegetables. Here are a few of my favorite recipes.

VEGETABLE COMBO

---

1 package frozen mixed vegetables
Water
3-oz. (84 g) package lemon-flavored gelatin
1 tbsp (15 ml) cider vinegar
¼ cup (60 ml) chopped green onion
¼ cup (60 ml) chopped green pepper
1 pimiento, diced

1. Cook vegetables in 1 cup (240 ml) boiling water. When tender, drain and dissolve the gelatin in the cooking liquid.
2. Add 1 cup (240 ml) cold water and the vinegar. Refrigerate until gelatin begins to set.
3. Add the cooked vegetables and the rest of the ingredients. Pour into individual molds and refrigerate until firm. Serve on lettuce with a mayonnaise or sour cream dressing.

EASY COTTAGE TOMATO ASPIC

2 cups (480 ml) tomato juice
3-oz. (84 g) package lemon-flavored gelatin
Few drops red pepper sauce
8-oz. (224 g) carton cream-style cottage cheese
¼ cup (60 ml) chopped celery
¼ cup (60 ml) chopped green pepper
¼ cup (60 ml) chopped green onion
¼ cup (60 ml) chopped cucumber

1. Heat 1 cup (240 ml) of the tomato juice to the boiling point. Stir in gelatin. Add rest of tomato juice, pepper sauce, and cottage cheese, stirring well to break up any lumps.
2. Refrigerate. When mixture begins to set, add other ingredients and pour into individual molds.
3. Refrigerate until firm. Serve on greens with mayonnaise, creamy Italian dressing, or sour cream.

CIDER SALAD

1 envelope unflavored gelatin
¼ cup (60 ml) cold water
1¾ cups (420 ml) cider or apple juice
½ stick cinnamon
3 cloves
1 unpeeled apple, cored and chopped
½ cup (120 ml) chopped celery
½ cup (120 ml) drained crushed pineapple

1.   Soften the gelatin in the water while you bring the cider to a boil with the cinnamon and cloves. Add the gelatin and stir. Put the cover on the pan and allow the cider to steep for 1 hour off the heat.

2.   Remove the spices and add the other ingredients. Refrigerate and stir once or twice until the mixture begins to thicken.

3.   Pour into molds and refrigerate. Serve on salad greens with mayonnaise.

MORE SUGGESTIONS FOR GELATIN MOLDS

Prepare flavored gelatin according to package directions. Substitute fruit juice or syrup for half of the water if possible. Try some of these combinations:

1. Drained frozen or fresh melon balls and canned pineapple tidbits in lemon-lime gelatin. This can also be served as a dessert in sherbet glasses.

2. Grated carrots and cabbage and drained crushed pineapple in lemon- or orange-flavored gelatin. This is called "sunshine salad" for obvious reasons.

3. Grapefruit sections in lemon- or lime-flavored gelatin made with grapefruit juice and ginger ale.

4. Pitted sweet cherries, sliced celery, and chopped nuts in orange- or lemon-flavored gelatin.

5. Diced apples and oranges, pineapple tidbits, sliced banana, and broken walnuts in lemon- or banana-flavored gelatin. Good for dessert too.

STICK-TO-THE-RIB STARCHES

Unless yours is a family of dieters, you will want to include a starchy dish and/or bread in your dinner menu. Many of the main-dish recipes earlier in this book include the starch. The following comments and suggestions are for serving starch as a separate dish.

POTATOES

Potatoes are, of course, nutrition-filled vegetables. They are included in this chapter rather than in the vegetable chapter to make meal planning easier. There are three main types of potatoes: new potatoes, which may be either red or brown and have very thin skins; baking, western, or Idaho potatoes; and plain "boiling" potatoes. Do not buy greenish, sprouted, or spotted potatoes. Buy only enough to last for a week or two. Store in a cool, dry place.

Baked Potatoes. Select large firm potatoes of uniform size. Scrub well with a stiff brush and cut out any blemishes. Prick a few holes in the skins with a fork. Rub the skins with butter or margarine and place directly on the oven rack, in a shallow pan, or on a special potato rack with spikes that go up into the potatoes. The spikes make the potatoes cook more quickly. Bake potatoes until soft at any convenient temperature from 325° to 450°F (160° to 230°C). Allow about an hour for medium-sized potatoes at 375°F (190°C). To test, pick up a potato in a towel or hot pad. Squeeze it gently. If it feels soft, it is done. Cut a cross in the top of the potato and push the ends toward the center to release the steam.

Serve with butter or with sour cream, which may be mixed with chopped onions or chives. A small pitcher of hot skimmed milk or yogurt may be substituted for anyone who wishes to reduce fat intake.

Boiled Potatoes. Wash well, remove any spots or sprouts, and pare. Leave whole or cut into pieces of the same size. Cook covered in a small amount of boiling salted water until tender —15 to 40 minutes depending on size. Drain well.

Serve with butter, salt, pepper, and chopped chives or parsley. Add a cream sauce or combine potatoes in a creamed sauce with cooked peas, mushrooms, or small white onions or with all three. These may be baked with a cheese topping.

Mashed Potatoes. Boil the potatoes as indicated above. Drain well and shake over heat for just a moment to be sure that all of the moisture is gone. Break the potatoes into pieces and mash with a potato masher or whip with a portable electric mixer, adding milk, butter, salt, and pepper until they are fluffy—not mushy. Taste and add more seasoning if necessary. Most cookbooks call for hot milk, a procedure that dirties an extra pan. I keep the potatoes over very low heat while I beat them with cold milk. You must work fast to prevent scorching, but you save a pan, which is worth a great deal if you are your own dishwasher.

Scalloped Potatoes. Wash, pare, and thinly slice potatoes until you have about 3 cups (720 ml). Put a layer of potatoes in a well-greased casserole, dot with butter, and sprinkle with flour. Repeat the layers until you have used up all of the potatoes, 2 tbsp (30 ml) flour, and about ¼ cup (60 ml) of butter. Pour 1¼ cups (300 ml) milk, mixed with 1 tsp (5 ml) salt, a little mustard, and freshly ground black pepper, over the top. Bake covered for 30 minutes in a 350°F (175°C) oven. Remove the cover and bake 1 hour. The temperature may be increased or decreased, depending on what else is in the oven with the potatoes.

Alternatively, you may prepare the potatoes as above but substitute 1 can condensed cream of mushroom, celery, or cheese soup for the flour and milk.

To vary: Before baking add sliced onion, chopped green onions, or chives, shredded or cubed cheese, crisply fried and crumbled bacon, cubed cooked ham, or pork.

POTATO SALAD

There must be as many ways to make potato salad as there are families in the United States. Each family is convinced that its way is *the* way.

4 medium-sized potatoes
3 tbsp (40 ml) French dressing
¼ cup (60 ml) chopped onions
Mayonnaise
Salt
Pepper

1. Early in the day boil the potatoes until tender. Cool and cut into large slices or cubes. Toss with French dressing and refrigerate covered, shaking occasionally, until about an hour before serving time.

2. An hour before serving time, mix with onions, enough mayonnaise to hold the mixture together, and salt and pepper to taste. Chill.

To vary: Add 2 hard-boiled eggs, ¼ cup (60 ml) chopped pickle, 2 tbsp (30 ml) chopped green pepper, ¼ cup (60 ml) chopped celery. Substitute sour cream for part of the mayonnaise. Add 1 tbsp (15 ml) prepared mustard.

PREPARED POTATOES—DRIED AND FROZEN

These are a great convenience. Furthermore, there are times during the year—usually in the spring—when "instant" mashed potatoes may be less expensive than the potatoes you cook and mash yourself. Some of the other mixes and frozen potatoes—especially french fries—may save you money. They will certainly save you time. Prepare according to package directions.

SWEET POTATOES OR YAMS

A yam by any name is sweeter, brighter, and moister than a sweet potato. Both are a rich source of vitamin A. They spoil rather quickly, so buy for one meal at a time.

Baked Sweet Potatoes. Prepare and bake just as you do white potatoes. Yams will take less time to bake.

Boiled Sweet Potatoes. Scrub well but do not skin. Drop in boiling salted water, cover, and cook until tender, about 20 minutes. Drain and skin.

To serve: Mash with butter and a little milk or orange juice and season with nutmeg, crushed pineapple, nuts, honey, or molasses, or cut in halves or quarters and toss with butter and brown sugar or butter and maple syrup.

Canned Sweet Potatoes and Yams are almost as good as fresh ones and are a convenient food to keep on hand. There is great variety among brands, so find one that you like and stick to it. Canned sweet potatoes may be prepared in any of the ways suggested for boiled sweet potatoes.

RICE

If you've never tried brown rice, do. It takes longer to cook than white rice, but it has a delicious "nutty" quality. Regular white rice is not difficult to cook and many people like it better than instant rice. Preflavored packaged rice is very expensive compared to the flavored rice you can make by simply adding a bouillon cube or broth and a few herbs.

Whatever type of rice you choose, cook it according to package directions.

To vary: Sauté chopped onion or green pepper in butter or margarine. Add the rice and stir until it is well coated with butter. Add water, broth, or tomato juice and cook according to package directions. Cook rice in poultry or meat broth or bouillon. When tender, season with lemon juice and grated lemon or orange peel. Cook rice in carrot, pineapple, orange, or tomato juice rather than water, or use vegetable cooking liquids. Season with curry powder, chili powder, nutmeg, seasoned salt, onion salt, garlic salt, seasoned pepper, or any other spice. Add lots of minced parsley. Add grated or shredded cheese. Add chopped cooked ham, poultry, fish, or crumbled crisp bacon. Add dried or fresh herbs suitable for the meat or fish being served. Combine with almost any cooked vegetable.

PASTA

Noodles, spaghetti, and macaroni can be used interchangeably. Again, read the instructions on the package and cook accordingly. There are lovely green noodles worth seeking.

Do you know how to get long spaghetti into a pot that is narrower than the length of the spaghetti? Bring the water and 1 tbsp (15 ml) vegetable oil to a boil. Put the spaghetti into the water with what won't fit sticking out. As the part in the water begins to soften, push the part that is sticking out down in. When you have worked all of the spaghetti into the water, stir it with a fork so that the individual pieces will separate.

Cook according to package directions and drain well. Do not overcook.

To vary: Toss with butter, a few tablespoons of milk and grated, shredded, or cubed cheese. Add a cream or cheese sauce. Top with butter and chopped chives, parsley, chopped pimiento, poppy seeds, or buttered croutons. Add sautéed onions or mushrooms.

MACARONI SALAD

1 cup (240 ml) uncooked macaroni—elbows or shells
2 hard-boiled eggs
1 cup (240 ml) chopped celery
¼ cup (60 ml) chopped onion
¼ cup (60 ml) chopped green pepper
1 pimiento, chopped
1 tbsp (15 ml) pickle juice or vinegar
½ tsp (2.5 ml) salt
Few grinds pepper
¼ tsp (1 ml) dry mustard
⅓ cup (80 ml) mayonnaise or salad dressing

1. Early in the day, or at least 3 hours before dinner, cook the macaroni according to package directions, and hard-boil the eggs.
2. Drain the macaroni, slice the eggs, and mix with the other ingredients.
3. Chill until serving time and unmold on greens.

BREADS

The Staff of Life has come in for a lot of attention lately. After many years when the only bread most Americans ate was soft, white, and lacking in vitamins, really good and nutritious breads are becoming widely available. Many of the so-called natural loaves are delicious. In addition to the variety of breads and rolls available on bakery shelves, there are also frozen breads, refrigerator rolls, and bread and roll mixes. Unless you are willing to dedicate a great deal of time to baking, you will probably depend on your supermarket to supply the bread for your family. Remember that bread freezes well. It makes sense, therefore, to keep loaves of several different kinds in your freezer. You can then remove just the slices you need at any given time and keep the rest frozen.

THE GRAND FINALE: DESSERTS

Dinner without dessert is like a hot dog without mustard —incomplete. There's nothing more to say on the subject except that the final course should be chosen to complement the rest of the meal. Choose a light dessert, if the main course has been heavy; a bland dessert if the main course has been spicy; a tart or crunchy dessert if the main course has been creamy.

FRUIT

When in doubt, choose fruit. Easiest of all is a bowl of fresh fruits, which can double as a centerpiece for your table. Picture a wooden bowl filled with bright red apples or a glass bowl with apples, oranges, bananas, and grapes. Consider also fresh, frozen, and canned fruits in combination. Following are suggestions for some interesting fruit cups:

1. Drain fruit cocktail or a combination of canned fruits— pineapple tidbits, pear slices, and mandarin oranges, for example. If convenient, add fresh fruit—sliced or diced banana, seeded or seedless grapes, orange sections, unpared apple or pear slices, or

melon balls. Place all of the fruits in a bowl, mixing well so that the banana, pear, or apple will not darken. Open a small container of frozen strawberries or raspberries. Place on top of the fruits and refrigerate. Stir again before serving. This is especially good if the berries are still slightly icy at serving time.

2. Top drained and chilled fruit cocktail or a combination of fruits with small scoops of fruit-flavored sherbet just before serving.

3. Top fruits with sour cream sprinkled with brown sugar, chopped candied ginger, or nuts.

4. Drain pear halves. Make a sauce by combining ¼ cup (60 ml) mint jelly with 2 tbsp (30 ml) pear syrup. Bring to boil and set aside. Just before serving, spoon lemon sherbet into dessert dishes. Top with pear halves and spoon mint sauce over the top.

5. Cut melons into serving-size wedges. Put a scoop of pineapple sherbet on each wedge. Top with blueberries, with the mint sauce given above, or with crème de menthe.

6. Drain canned peach halves. Make a sauce by combining red raspberry jam and water and heating until smooth. Put a scoop of vanilla ice cream in each peach half and top with sauce.

7. Top drained pear halves or sliced bananas with vanilla ice cream and chocolate sauce.

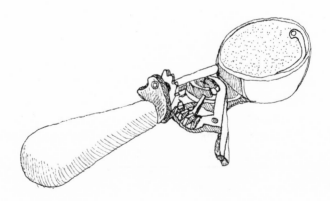

MERRY BERRY

8-oz. (224-g) package frozen raspberries or strawberries
1 cup (240 ml) liquid
3-oz. (84-g) package raspberry- or strawberry-flavored
  gelatin
2 cups (1 pint) (480 ml) vanilla or strawberry ice cream
Whipped cream or whipped-cream substitute (optional)

1. Thaw and drain berries. Pour berry juice into measuring cup and add enough water to make 1 cup (240 ml). Bring to a boil, remove from heat, and stir in gelatin.
2. When gelatin is dissolved, add ice cream, stirring until smooth. Add drained berries and blend.
3. Pour into parfait glasses or dessert dishes and chill in refrigerator—*not* the freezer—until set, about an hour. Top with whipped cream just before serving if you like.

This is a perfect party dessert because it is good, unusually pretty, and can be made a day in advance. It also makes a delicious pie. When you have prepared the mixture, pour into a baked or crumb pie shell. Top with whipped cream just before serving.

FRUIT CRISP

1 can apple, cherry, blueberry, strawberry, or peach
  pie filling
¼ cup (60 ml) butter or margarine
½ cup (120 ml) sugar
½ cup (120 ml) flour
½ cup (120 ml) quick-cooking oatmeal
¼ tsp (1 ml) cinnamon

1.   Empty pie filling into a greased 8- or 9-inch (20 or 22.5 cm) pie plate.
2.   Melt butter and combine with the rest of the ingredients. Sprinkle over the pie filling.
3.   Bake 30 minutes in a 350°F (175°C) oven. Serve warm or cold with ice cream, whipped cream, or whipped-cream substitute. May be reheated in the oven if desired.

ICE CREAM

The basic American dessert is surely ice cream—or ice milk. If you're bored with chocolate, strawberry, and vanilla, try some of these toppings or combinations:

1.   Chocolate sauce may be made by melting a 6-oz. (188-g) package of semisweet chocolate pieces with 1 tbsp (15 ml) butter and ¼ cup (60 ml) milk or cream.
2.   Melt ¼ cup (60 ml) peanut butter with the chocolate sauce ingredients above.
3.   Fruit sauces may be made by heating jam with a little water and stirring until smooth, or by cooking a package of frozen fruit with 1 tsp (5 ml) of cornstarch mixed with 1 tbsp (15 ml) of cold water.

4. Heated maple syrup, pancake syrup, or honey makes a delicious topping, especially for nut ice creams.

5. If you like the crunch of nuts on a sundae but not the fat, try topping your sundae with crispy cereal.

6. Sprinkle nutmeg on chocolate or vanilla ice cream.

ICE CREAM PIE

---

6 oz. (188 g) package semisweet chocolate pieces

3 tbsp (45 ml) butter or margarine

2½ cups (600 ml) crisp rice cereal

1 quart (.95 l) coffee, mint, or butter pecan ice cream

Bitter chocolate (optional)

1. Melt the chocolate pieces and butter. Stir in the cereal. Press into the bottom and sides of a 9-inch (22.9 cm) pie plate. Refrigerate an hour or so.

2. Remove the ice cream from the freezer to allow to soften a bit. Spoon into the cooled pie shell, pressing down with the back of the spoon. Dip the spoon into hot water and smooth out the top of the pie. Grate bitter chocolate over the top of the pie.

3. Cut with a sharp knife into 6 pieces. Freeze. Remove the pieces 15 minutes before you expect to serve them.

PUDDINGS AND CUSTARDS

Packaged pudding mixes are a godsend to busy people. They come in many flavors and can be prepared in minutes. They can also be poured into crumb shells, from the store or made according to the recipe on the graham cracker box. Following are a few suggestions for adding interest to packaged puddings:

1.   Add 1 tbsp (15 ml) of instant coffee powder to 1 package of vanilla pudding mix. Cook according to package directions. Or substitute chilled strong coffee for the water in instant mix. Also make up 1 package of chocolate pudding. Layer the puddings in parfait glasses or alternate them in small glass dishes and run a knife through them for a marbled effect. Refrigerate and serve with whipped topping. This is called "Coco Mocha."
2.   Layer or marble vanilla pudding with fruit jam.
3.   Mix up a package of vanilla pudding mix. Pour a little of it on the bottom of a crumb crust. Top with sliced bananas and pour the rest of the pudding on the top.
4.   Sprinkle grated coconut on the top of pudding.

BAKED CUSTARD

This makes a delicious and nutritious dessert or breakfast dish. The only tricky part is trying to decide when the custard is done.

3 cups (720 ml) milk
3 eggs
½ cup (120 ml) sugar
½ tsp (2.5 ml) salt
1 tsp vanilla
Dash nutmeg

1. Scald the milk. In other words, put it in a pan over low heat until bubbles form around the edge of the milk and steam rises from it. Do not let it come to a full boil.

2. In the meantime, stir together the eggs, sugar, and salt. Mix in the hot milk and vanilla and combine well.

3. Pour into 5 or 6 slightly greased custard cups and sprinkle with nutmeg. Put a paper towel in the bottom of a baking dish large enough to hold the custard cups. Put the cups on top of the towel and pour boiling water—about 1 inch (2.5 cm) deep— around the cups.

4. Place in the oven set at any temperature between 325° and 425°F (160° and 220°C). Bake 20 minutes to 1 hour depending on the temperature. Once you've made custards you won't have any trouble deciding when they are done. The first time, it's a problem. When you tap them, the tops should look firm, not runny. If you put a table knife down into the custard near the center, it will come out with liquid on it until the custard is done. When it is done, the knife will either have little pieces of custard on it or it will come out clean. Serve hot or cold.

RICH RICE PUDDING

This is another, much heartier, dessert that may also be served for breakfast. The recipe makes 6 to 8 servings but it will stay fresh in the refrigerator for several days.

2 cups (480 ml) cooked brown or white rice
2½ cups (600 ml) milk
¼ cup (60 ml) dry milk
4 eggs, lightly beaten
¼ cup (60 ml) honey
1 cup (240 ml) raisins
½ tsp (2.5 ml) grated orange peel (optional)
½ tsp (2.5 ml) cinnamon (optional)
¼ tsp (1 ml) salt

1.   Combine all of the ingredients and cook over *very* low heat, stirring frequently until the mixture begins to thicken, about 10 minutes.
2.   Then stir constantly until the mixture is pudding-thick. Serve hot or cold.

CAKE

There are several ways to provide cake for your family. One is to buy it fresh or frozen. Another is to make it from a mix. Finally you can make it from scratch. I am including only one basic cake recipe. In all honesty I must tell you that it will never win a prize at the county fair because its texture is not fine enough, but it is far less expensive than any cake you can buy and just as fast as any mix. If you have a blender you can prepare it for the oven in less than 5 minutes. If you don't have a blender it will take only slightly longer. It's a small, single layer cake, moist and very tasty.

BASIC FASTER-THAN-A-MIX CAKE

¼ cup (60 ml) margarine
¾ cup (180 ml) sugar
2 eggs
½ cup (120 ml) milk
1 tsp (5 ml) vanilla
1 cup (240 ml) flour
2 tsp (10 ml) baking powder
¼ tsp (1 ml) salt

1.   Put margarine, sugar, eggs, milk, and vanilla in the blender container. Blend, uncovered, at high speed for 30 seconds (just count slowly to 30). Turn off the motor and scrape the sides of the container.

2.   Add the flour (you don't need to bother sifting it), baking powder, and salt. Turn the blender to high speed for no more than 3 seconds. Turn off and stir the contents with a rubber scraper, pushing any of the flour that is around the edges down into the liquid. Blend for another few seconds, turn off and use the scraper again. Continue this blend-scrape operation until the batter is smooth, no longer. It is important to blend as little as possible after the flour has been added.

3.   Pour the batter into a well-greased 8-inch (20 cm) square or 9-inch (22.5 cm) round bake pan. Place in 350°F (175°C) oven and bake 20 to 25 minutes until the top is lightly browned and the cake springs back when you lightly press your finger into the top center. Another way to test for doneness is to insert a cake tester or thin metal skewer into the middle of the cake. If it comes out dry, the cake is done. It is also done when it begins to pull away from the sides of the pan. Cool on a rack. See suggested toppings below.

If you don't have a blender, soften the margarine first. You can do this by leaving the margarine at room temperature for an hour or so. Or you can measure it and put it in an *oven-proof* mixing bowl and set the bowl in the oven while you are pre-heating it until the margarine begins to be runny. Add the sugar, eggs, milk, and vanilla and mix well with a rotary beater (electric or hand) for 2 minutes. Add the flour mixed with the baking powder and salt and beat for another 2 minutes. Continue as for the blender cake.

UPSIDE-DOWN CAKE

¼ cup (60 ml) margarine
¼ cup (60 ml) brown sugar
A few shakes of cinnamon
2 medium-sized apples peeled and sliced, or slices of canned pineapple or peaches
Nuts (optional)
Maraschino cherries (optional)
Basic cake batter

1.   Melt margarine in a 9-inch (22.5 cm) round cake pan. (Place the pan over very low heat or put it in the preheating oven for a few minutes to melt the margarine.) Tilt the pan to spread the margarine evenly.
2.   Sprinkle with brown sugar and cinnamon.
3.   Lay apple or pineapple or peach slices in an attractive pattern over the brown sugar. Do not overlap the fruit. Fill in the spaces with nuts or cherries if you like.
4.   Pour the batter over the fruit and bake as indicated in the basic recipe.
5.   Cool in the pan for 10 minutes and then run a knife around the inside of the pan to loosen the cake. Put a plate upside down on top of the cake pan and invert so that the pan is upside down on the plate. Remove the pan. If any of the brown sugar goo sticks to the pan just scrape it out and return it to the cake.

CHOCOLATE CAKE

¼ cup (60 ml) cocoa
Basic cake batter

Add cocoa with the sugar to basic cake batter.

SPICE CAKE

½ tsp (2.5 ml) cinnamon
¼ tsp (1 ml) cloves
¼ tsp (1 ml) nutmeg
Basic cake batter
½ cup (120 ml) raisins (optional)
½ cup (120 ml) nut meats (optional)

Stir spices into the flour and add to basic cake batter. Stir raisins or nuts into the batter just before it goes into the baking pan.

ORANGE OR LEMON CAKE

1 orange or 1 lemon
Basic cake batter

Rub an orange or lemon across the small holes in a grater. Try to grate as much of the brightly colored part of the skin and as little of the white under part of the skin as possible. Cut the fruit in half and extract as much juice as possible. Discard pits. Pour the juice into a measuring cup and add milk to make ½ cup (120 ml). Use this liquid instead of the milk called for in the basic cake recipe. Add the peel with the liquid.

CAKE TOPPINGS

These toppings may be used on the cake and variations above or on any other cake. If you use a standard cake mix, either double the amounts for any of the toppings below or bake the cake in two pans and put one topping on the cake in one pan and another topping on the cake baked in the other pan.

SIMPLE SUGAR

2 tbsp (30 ml) granulated or powdered sugar

Sprinkle over a hot cake and allow to cool.

SIMPLE FROSTING

2 tbsp (30 ml) margarine
2 tbsp (30 ml) milk or cream
½ tsp (2.5 ml) vanilla
Powdered sugar—about half of a 1-lb. (224 g) box

Melt margarine and add milk and vanilla. Beat in powdered sugar, a little at a time, until the frosting is thick and spreadable. Spread on a cooled cake.

To vary: Add 2 tbsp (30 ml) cocoa with the sugar or substitute orange or lemon juice for the milk.

WHIPPED TOPPING

½ cup (120 ml) ground-up peanut brittle, hard mints, or candy canes
1 cup (240 ml) whipped topping

Stir candy into topping and spoon onto wedges of plain cake.

CHOCOLATE MINT

Chocolate-coated candy mints

Place mint wafers in a single layer—close together but not touching—on a hot cake. Return the cake to the oven just until the wafers begin to melt. Smooth the melting goo over the cake and cool.

COTTAGE PUDDING SAUCE

¼ cup (60 ml) sugar
1½ tsp (7.5 ml) cornstarch
½ cup (120 ml) water
¼ cup (60 ml) grated lemon rind
2 tbsp (30 ml) butter or margarine
1 tbsp (15 ml) lemon juice
Shake of nutmeg

Combine sugar and cornstarch in a small saucepan. Add water, rind, and stir over moderate heat until the sauce boils and thickens. Remove from the heat and add butter, juice, and nutmeg. Serve warm or cold over wedges of cake.

LAZY DAISY TOPPING

¼ cup (60 ml) melted butter or margarine
¼ cup (60 ml) brown sugar
3 tbsp (45 ml) cream or milk
¾ cup (180 ml) chopped nuts or coconut or a combination
    of the two

Combine all of these ingredients and spread on warm cake. Put under the broiler until lightly browned. Watch carefully as the topping will burn in an incredibly short time.

SHORT CAKE

Sugared berries or other fresh or thawed frozen fruit
Whipped cream, ice cream, or whipped topping

Split wedges of cake and top with fruit and cream.

BOSTON CREAM PIE

1 package vanilla pudding and pie filling mix prepared according to package directions for pie

½ cup (120 ml) semisweet chocolate pieces

2 tbsp (30 ml) milk

Split a single layer of cool cake crosswise to make two layers. Spread cooled pudding mix between the layers. Melt chocolate pieces and milk. Pour over top of the cake.

COOKIES

Cookies disappear so quickly at my house that it seldom seems worthwhile to bake them. Of course they are delicious. That's why we can't keep them on hand. Even our dog prefers home-made cookies. Fortunately he can't reach the cookie jar, but everyone else takes a cookie each time he or she walks by the jar.

Here, you will find only two cookie recipes. The first one is incredibly simple and yummy—almost a candy. The next is for cookies so nutritious that you can eat them for breakfast with a clear conscience.

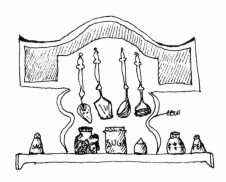

CRUNCHIES

6-oz. (168-g) package chocolate bits
3 cups (720 ml) Chinese noodles or rice cereal, or a combination of the two

1. Melt chocolate in the top of a double boiler over water. Stir in noodles or cereal.
2. Mix well and press into a buttered 9-inch-square (22.5 cm) pan. Refrigerate and cut into squares.

CEREAL CRUNCH COOKIES

1 cup (240 ml) vegetable shortening
1 cup (240 ml) white sugar
1 cup (240 ml) dark brown sugar, packed
3 eggs
2 tsp (10 ml) vanilla
2 cups (480 ml) sifted all-purpose flour
1 tsp (5 ml) baking soda
1 tsp (5 ml) baking powder
¾ tsp (4 ml) salt
2 cups (480 ml) rolled oats
1 cup (240 ml) rice cereal, grapenuts, granola or a combination.
⅓ cup (80 ml) dry milk
⅓ cup (80 ml) wheat germ

1. Cream shortening and sugar. Add eggs and vanilla.
2. Add flour, which has been sifted with baking soda, baking powder, and salt. Mix. Add the rest of the ingredients.
3. Drop the stiff dough by heaped teaspoons onto greased cookie sheets, leaving 2 inches between cookies. Bake in 350°F (175°C) oven for 10 minutes or until golden. Makes about 75 large cookies. Store in airtight containers.

To vary: Add raisins, semisweet chocolate pieces, or nuts.

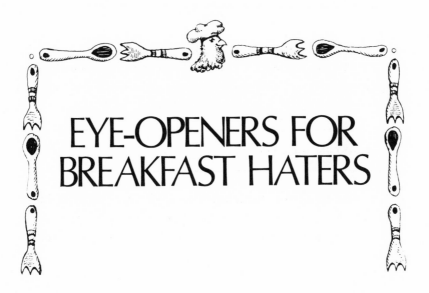

EYE-OPENERS FOR BREAKFAST HATERS

What's your excuse for not eating breakfast? You don't have time? It's a bore? You're dieting? You may be able to convince your mind that you don't need breakfast, but you can't convince your body. It needs nourishment—particularly protein—to keep going until lunch.

The following suggestions are for nutritious breakfasts that you can make for yourself in a matter of minutes. I don't think you'll find them boring either. Nowhere have I mentioned bacon, eggs, and toast, or cereal, milk, and orange juice. (A further word about orange juice. You need it or another source of vitamin C—other citrus fruits, melon, berries, or tomatoes—but not necessarily in the morning. If you'd rather consume your vitamin C with lunch or at snack time, fine.)

FRUIT AND . . .

If you have absolutely no time to eat, drop an apple, several slices of Cheddar or Swiss cheese, and crackers or whole wheat melba toast slices in a paper bag and eat on the run. If you have just a minute to sit down to eat, top fresh or canned fruit with cottage cheese. Eat with or without toasted raisin bread or an English muffin.

BREAKFAST-IN-A-GLASS

All of the following breakfasts-in-a-glass may be considered complete in themselves; if you are neither a 90-pound-weakling nor a dieter, you will want to add muffins, toast, or breakfast rolls.

ORANGE SPECIAL

1 small raw carrot cut into rounds
1 canned peach half
½ cup (120 ml) orange juice
¼ cup (60 ml) peach syrup
½ cup (120 ml) plain yogurt
1 ice cube

Put everything in the blender jar and blend at top speed until mixture is creamy.

EGGNOG

1 egg
1 cup (240 ml) milk
2 tbsp (30 ml) dry milk
¼ tsp (1 ml) salt
¼ tsp (1 ml) vanilla
1 tsp (5 ml) sugar or honey
Dash of nutmeg (optional)

Mix all the ingredients together in the blender or with a rotary beater. Pour into a glass and sprinkle nutmeg on top.

MILK SHAKES

1 egg
½ cup (120 ml) any flavor of ice cream or ice milk
1 cup (240 ml) milk
2 tbsp (30 ml) dry milk

Put all of the ingredients in the blender jar and blend until smooth.

To vary: Add 2 tbsp (30 ml) peanut butter with vanilla ice cream, a whole banana with chocolate ice cream, a few canned apricot halves with lemon ice cream, or substitute orange juice for part of the milk.

SANDWICHES FOR BREAKFAST?

Why not? Try egg salad sandwiches (chopped hard-cooked egg, mixed with onion salt and mayonnaise), toasted cheese with or without crisply fried bacon or tomato slices, cream cheese topped with jam and chopped nuts; peanut butter and sliced banana; any cold meat or fish you have on hand.

OR DESSERT?

In the dessert chapter of this book you will find recipes for three fantastically nutritious sweets: rice pudding, baked custard, and cereal cookies. The rice pudding is hearty enough to provide a complete breakfast for the small eater. Eat the custard with toast or muffins, and the cookies with fruit and a large glass of milk.

It takes a little time to measure and mix the ingredients for these muffins, but once that's done you'll have about a gallon of batter. Supposedly, this batter will be good forever. I can't guarantee its lasting quality because we've always eaten the whole batch in less than three weeks. If you have a little time, you can just pour the batter into muffin tins and bake fresh muffins in the morning. If not, you can make a batch of toaster muffins (see page 108) at any time and store them in your freezer.

If you want to make them even better and more healthful, add raisins or nuts just before you bake them.

HEALTH MUFFINS TO SERVE AGAIN AND AGAIN AND AGAIN

6 cups (1.4 l) shredded whole bran cereal
2 cups (480 ml) boiling water
3 cups (720 ml) sugar
1 cup (240 ml) solid shortening
4 eggs
1 cup (240 ml) wheat germ
5 cups (1.2 l) flour—use all regular white flour or 3 cups (720 ml) white flour and 2 cups (480 ml) whole wheat flour
1 tsp (5 ml) salt
2 tbsp (30 ml) baking soda
1 quart (.95 l) buttermilk

1.   Put bran in a large mixing bowl. Pour the boiling water over the bran and set aside.

2.   Take out the largest bowl or soup pot in your kitchen. In it, beat together the sugar, shortening, and eggs. Add the wheat germ.

3. Sift the flours and the baking soda and salt together in another bowl or on a large sheet of wax paper.

4. Add about a cup of the flour mixture and ½ cup (120 ml) buttermilk to the egg mixture and beat. Continue to add flour and buttermilk, beating after each addition until they have been incorporated into the mixture in the huge container.

5. Stir in the bran mix.

6. Store in covered jars in the refrigerator.

7. To bake, preheat the oven to 400°F (200°C). Spoon the batter into well-greased muffin tins (or use paper muffin cups in the tin). Each cup should be no more than half-filled as the batter will rise as it bakes. One quart of batter makes at least a dozen large muffins. Bake 20 to 25 minutes until the muffins are firm when you press the top of them with your finger.

You may also make toaster muffins from this batter. Spoon ¼ cup (60 ml) of batter onto a well-greased cookie sheet and spread out to make a circle about 3 inches in diameter. The batter will spread further so place the muffins at least 2 inches apart. Bake at 400°F (200°C) until firm, about 15 minutes. Cool thoroughly. Stack the muffins with a piece of wax paper between each of them and place in a tightly sealed plastic bag. Freeze. Remove from the freezer as many muffins as you wish to eat at one time and place them, while still frozen, in the toaster at a "light" setting.

BEYOND THE PEANUT BUTTER SANDWICH

Two teen-agers ate together regularly. Every noon, one of them took out his sandwich, opened it, and scowled, "Peanut butter! I hate peanut butter!"

This went on for days until his friend finally asked, "Why don't you tell your mother you don't like peanut butter?"

"You leave my mother out of this," said the peanut butter hater indignantly. "I make my own sandwiches."

It's an old joke, but it illustrates the fact that many of us are in a lunchtime rut. We fix the same old sandwich day after day because it takes so little time and thought. Then we complain that our lunches are boring. Here are a few suggestions for more interesting lunches.

SOME JAZZY SANDWICHES

1. Mix together a 3-oz. (84 g) package cream cheese, 1 tbsp (15 ml) bottled chutney, ¼ to ½ tsp (1 to 2.5 ml) curry powder (depending on your taste and the strength of the curry), 1 tbsp

(15 ml) lemon juice, and 1 chopped apple. Spread on raisin bread. Or add raisins to the mixture and spread on brown or white bread.

2.   Drain an 8-oz. (224 g) can of crushed pineapple. Mix pineapple with cream-style cottage cheese. Spread on any kind of bread. Store leftover mixture in the refrigerator to use within a few days.

3.   Cut cooked chicken or turkey into small cubes. Add ¼ cup (60 ml) peanuts or roasted soy beans to 1 cup (240 ml) chicken. Moisten with mayonnaise. Spread between slices of white or brown bread. Freeze, if you like.

4.   Add well-drained spiced apple slices to ham and cheese sandwiches.

5.   Put 1 cup (240 ml) of dates—with pits removed—into blender jar with 2 tbsp (30 ml) orange or pineapple juice. Blend until chopped and spreadable. Add nuts if you like. Spread on the bread of your choice.

6.   Mix together a 3-oz. (84 g) package softened cream cheese, an 8-oz. (224 g) roll of liverwurst (at room temperature), 1 tbsp (15 ml) mayonnaise, 1 tbsp (15 ml) Worcestershire sauce, and 1 tbsp (15 ml) pickle relish. Spread on white, brown, or rye bread. This mixture may be stored up to 2 weeks in the refrigerator.

SEVEN SANDWICH SUBSTITUTES
AND LUNCH BAG ADDITIONS

1.   For a real quickie, just drop a banana and a few breakfast or granola bars into a bag.

2.   Freeze small cans of juice. Put in a plastic bag and then into a lunch bag along with a container of yogurt and a plastic spoon. The thawing juice will keep the yogurt cool.

3.   Spread peanut butter between leaves of lettuce. Roll and wrap in plastic.

4.   Put in a plastic bag strips of green pepper, cucumber, and carrots; whole cherry tomatoes and radishes; and cauliflower flowerettes. Sprinkle with a little salt and close tightly.

5.   Cover one side of a thin slice of ham with blue cheese spread. Put a well-drained spear of cooked asparagus on one end of the ham slice and roll tightly. Wrap in plastic.

6.   Stuff celery with cheese.

7.   Make a plastic packet of dried fruits, nuts, and roasted seeds.

INDEX

ABOUT
THE AUTHOR

LouAnn Gaeddert is a free-lance writer, a wife, and the mother of two teen-agers. Her daughter, Martha, is a particularly able cook who served as an advisor for this book. Mrs. Gaeddert is also the author of an adult cookbook, and five other books for young people. She lives in New York City.